JASON JANSSON

Divine Energy: The 7 Pillars of Awakening Kundalini

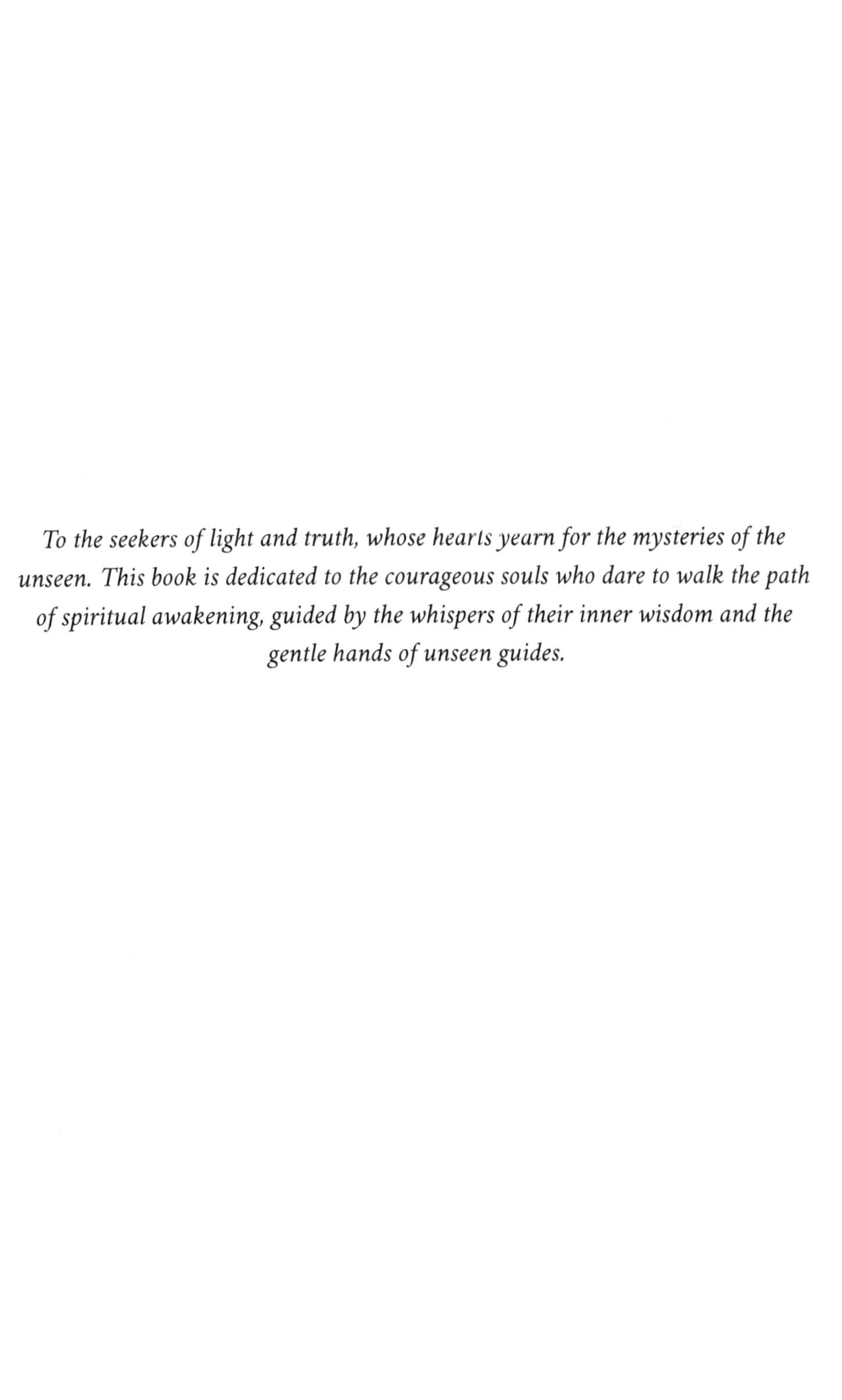

To the seekers of light and truth, whose hearts yearn for the mysteries of the unseen. This book is dedicated to the courageous souls who dare to walk the path of spiritual awakening, guided by the whispers of their inner wisdom and the gentle hands of unseen guides.

"In the spiritual journey, it's not about the destination but the transformation that happens within us as we walk the path."

Contents

Preface

In the journey of life, there comes a time when the familiar paths no longer suffice, and the soul yearns for something deeper, something more profound. This book is born from such a yearning—a desire to explore the mysteries of the spiritual realm, to connect with the divine within and around us, and to find meaning in the interconnectedness of all things. It is a guide for seekers, for those who feel the pull of the unseen and the call of the soul's awakening.

Throughout the ages, countless souls have embarked on this sacred journey, guided by the light of their inner wisdom and the support of like-minded companions. They have traversed the realms of meditation, breathwork, visualization, and community, each step bringing them closer to the truth that lies at the heart of existence. This book seeks to illuminate these paths, offering insights and practices that can help you connect with your deepest self and the divine source of all creation.

The chapters that follow are structured around seven pillars, each representing a fundamental aspect of spiritual growth and transformation. From the quiet depths of meditation and mindfulness to the powerful currents of community and support, these pillars provide a foundation upon which to build a life of spiritual awareness and fulfillment. Each chapter is a doorway into a different aspect of the spiritual journey, offering practical guidance, profound wisdom, and inspiring examples to help you on your path.

This book is not just a collection of teachings and practices; it is an invitation to embark on a journey of self-discovery and spiritual awakening. It is a call to step into the unknown, to trust in the process of transformation, and to embrace the challenges and joys of the spiritual path. Whether you are just beginning your journey or are well along the way, this book offers a companion for your soul, a guide to help you navigate the twists and turns of the spiritual landscape.

As you read these pages, may you find the guidance and inspiration you seek. May you connect with the divine light within you, and may you discover the boundless potential that resides in your heart and soul. This book is dedicated to your journey, to the unfolding of your spiritual path, and to the awakening of your true self. May it serve as a beacon of light, guiding you home to the sacred truth that lies within.

Welcome, seeker of truth and enlightenment, to a journey that transcends the mundane and delves into the mystical realms of divine energy and spiritual awakening. "Divine Energy: Seven Pillars for Spiritual Awakening and Kundalini Activation" is not just a book; it is a beacon of light guiding you towards a profound transformation, an awakening of the sacred energy that resides within you.

Imagine, if you will, a world where your spirit soars, untethered by the limitations of the physical realm. This is the world that awaits you as you embark on this sacred journey. The ancient sages and mystics spoke of a dormant energy, coiled like a serpent at the base of the spine, known as Kundalini. This potent force, when awakened, rises through the chakras, unlocking boundless wisdom, unearthly serenity, and a connection to the divine that transcends human comprehension.

Why should you read further? Because within these pages lie the keys to unlocking this extraordinary power. Each chapter unveils one of the seven foundational pillars that form the bedrock of Kundalini activation and spiritual awakening. These pillars are not mere concepts but living practices, each imbued with the potential to transform your life in ways you have never imagined.

The first pillar, Meditation and Mindfulness, invites you to dive into the ancient practice of meditation, where stillness speaks and the soul finds its true voice. Through techniques that quiet the mind, you will learn to allow the whispers of the divine to guide you. Meditation opens a gateway to profound inner peace, fostering a deep connection with your higher self and the universe.

The second pillar, Breathwork and Pranayama, explores the sacred art of breath control. Each inhale draws in the universe's life force, and each exhale releases what no longer serves you. Pranayama practices cleanse both your body and spirit, preparing you for the rise of Kundalini. Through breathwork, you will learn to harness and direct your energy, facilitating a smoother and more powerful awakening process.

In the third pillar, Physical Asanas and Movement, you will embrace the power of physical movement to awaken and align your energies. Specific Kundalini yoga poses, designed to strengthen the body and prepare it to channel divine energy, will be introduced. Movement becomes a meditative practice, uniting body, mind, and spirit in a harmonious dance that supports your spiritual growth.

The fourth pillar, Diet and Nutrition, unveils the secrets of spiritual nutrition, where food is not just sustenance but a pathway to enlightenment. You will discover diets and practices that support and enhance your spiritual journey. By nourishing your body with the right foods, you create a foundation for a healthy and vibrant energy flow, essential for sustaining Kundalini activation.

The fifth pillar, Sound and Mantras, immerses you in the transformative power of sound. Ancient mantras and chants, resonating with your soul, facilitate the awakening of your inner serpent. Sound healing practices will be explored, demonstrating how vibrations can cleanse and elevate your energetic state, making way for deeper spiritual experiences.

In the sixth pillar, Visualization and Intention Setting, you will harness the power of your mind through visualization and intention setting. Manifesting your spiritual goals and drawing closer to the divine becomes possible through focused mental practices. Visualization techniques will guide you in creating a vivid and compelling vision of your spiritual aspirations, while intention setting helps you stay aligned with your higher purpose.

The seventh and final pillar, Community and Support, underscores the importance of a spiritual community. You will learn how to find like-minded individuals who will support and elevate your journey, creating a network of light that amplifies your own. The strength of a community lies in its ability to provide guidance, encouragement, and shared wisdom, fostering a collective environment where spiritual growth flourishes.

As you turn each page, you will feel the mystical energies beginning to stir within you. This book is a portal, a sacred text that bridges the ancient wisdom of the past with the pressing spiritual needs of the present. You are not alone in this journey. Thousands have walked this path before you, and many more will follow. The transformation you seek is not only possible but inevitable when you commit to these practices with an open heart and a willing spirit.

So, dear reader, step into the unknown with courage and curiosity. Allow the teachings within "Divine Energy: Seven Pillars for Spiritual Awakening and Kundalini Activation" to guide you towards the light, awakening the divine energy within, and leading you to a state of being that is both enlightened and eternally connected to the source of all existence. Welcome to your awakening. The journey begins now.

Welcome to your awakening. The journey begins now.

In the vast tapestry of existence, where the mundane and the mystical intertwine, lies the extraordinary journey of spiritual awakening. The purpose of "Divine Energy: Seven Pillars for Spiritual Awakening and Kundalini Activation" is to serve as a luminous guide on this sacred path, illuminating the way with ancient wisdom and practical teachings. This book is not merely an assembly of words; it is a beacon of light designed to ignite the dormant energies within you, propelling you towards a state of divine consciousness and profound self-realization.

Imagine yourself standing at the threshold of a grand temple, its doors carved with symbols of ancient wisdom, beckoning you to enter. Within these hallowed halls, each chapter of this book serves as a pillar, supporting the edifice of your spiritual journey. These seven pillars—Meditation and

Mindfulness, Breathwork and Pranayama, Physical Asanas and Movement, Diet and Nutrition, Sound and Mantras, Visualization and Intention Setting, and Community and Support—are the foundational elements that will guide you towards the awakening of your Kundalini energy.

The purpose of this book is multifaceted. Firstly, it aims to demystify the complex and often esoteric teachings of Kundalini yoga. Through detailed descriptions and relatable examples, it bridges the gap between ancient traditions and contemporary understanding. For instance, when discussing Meditation and Mindfulness, the book does not merely present these practices as abstract concepts. Instead, it delves into the transformative power of sitting in stillness, illustrating how a few minutes of daily meditation can quiet the chaotic mind and open the heart to divine whispers.

Breathwork and Pranayama are explored not just as breathing exercises but as sacred rituals that connect you to the very essence of life. Picture yourself engaging in a simple yet profound practice of pranayama, each breath drawing in the life force of the universe, filling your being with vitality and peace. These practices are designed to cleanse and prepare your body and spirit, paving the way for the rise of Kundalini.

The book also emphasizes the importance of Physical Asanas and Movement. Through vivid descriptions, you will learn how specific yoga poses can align your energies and strengthen your physical vessel. Imagine moving through a series of asanas, each one a dance with the divine, your body becoming a conduit for the flow of spiritual energy.

Diet and Nutrition are presented not just as dietary recommendations but as an integral part of your spiritual practice. Visualize yourself consuming foods that nourish not only your body but also your soul, each meal a sacrament that brings you closer to the divine. The book offers practical advice and recipes that support this holistic approach to nutrition.

Sound and Mantras are explored through the lens of vibrational healing. Envision chanting ancient mantras, each syllable resonating through your being, dissolving negativity, and elevating your consciousness. The transformative power of sound is a key element in awakening the Kundalini energy within.

Visualization and Intention Setting are tools for manifesting your spiritual goals. Through guided visualization exercises, you will learn to create a vivid and compelling vision of your spiritual aspirations. Picture yourself setting clear intentions, each one a seed planted in the fertile ground of your consciousness, destined to bloom into reality.

Finally, the book underscores the importance of Community and Support. It guides you in finding a spiritual community that nurtures your growth, offering examples of how collective energy can amplify individual efforts. Imagine being surrounded by like-minded individuals, each one a beacon of light, together creating a network of support that elevates everyone involved.

In essence, the purpose of "Divine Energy: Seven Pillars for Spiritual Awakening and Kundalini Activation" is to provide you with a comprehensive and accessible guide to your spiritual journey. It seeks to inspire and empower you, offering practical tools and timeless wisdom to awaken the divine energy within. As you delve into these teachings, you will not only transform your own life but also contribute to the collective awakening of humanity, stepping into your true power as a radiant being of light.

The goal of "Divine Energy: Seven Pillars for Spiritual Awakening and Kundalini Activation" is to serve as a transformative guide, illuminating the path towards spiritual awakening and the activation of your inner Kundalini energy. This book is designed to be a companion on your spiritual journey, offering a blend of ancient wisdom and modern practices that demystify the esoteric and make the sublime accessible. At its core, this book seeks to inspire and empower you to unlock the boundless potential that resides within, guiding you through a comprehensive, step-by-step process that awakens your divine energy and connects you to the higher realms of consciousness.

Imagine standing at the precipice of a grand adventure, not in a distant land, but within the very depths of your own being. This journey leads to the core of your existence, where the sacred energy of Kundalini lies dormant, like a coiled serpent at the base of your spine. The awakening of this energy is akin to igniting a divine spark, a transformative process that elevates your consciousness, illuminates your spirit, and harmonizes your body and mind. This book's goal is to meticulously guide you through this profound awakening, ensuring you are equipped with the knowledge and practices necessary to safely and effectively awaken this potent force.

The path to awakening is structured around seven foundational pillars, each representing a crucial aspect of the journey. The first pillar, Meditation and Mindfulness, is your gateway to inner stillness. Through vivid descriptions and practical exercises, you will learn how to quiet the mind and open the heart, allowing the whispers of the divine to guide you. This chapter emphasizes the transformative power of meditation, illustrating how a few minutes of daily practice can lead to profound peace and spiritual clarity.

Breathwork and Pranayama, the second pillar, delves into the sacred art of breath control. Each breath you take is a conduit for life force energy, and mastering your breath is key to unlocking your inner power. Through detailed instructions and relatable examples, you will explore various pranayama techniques that cleanse the body and spirit, preparing you for the rise of Kundalini. This pillar highlights how conscious breathing can serve as a bridge between the physical and spiritual realms, facilitating a deeper connection to the divine.

The third pillar, Physical Asanas and Movement, guides you through the physical postures of Kundalini yoga. These asanas are not mere exercises but spiritual practices that prepare your body to channel divine energy. Imagine moving through a series of poses, each one designed to align your chakras and strengthen your physical vessel, making it a fit container for the awakening Kundalini. This chapter underscores the importance of physical health and alignment in supporting your spiritual journey.

Diet and Nutrition, the fourth pillar, explores the intricate relationship between what you consume and your spiritual well-being. The food you eat can either nourish your spiritual energy or hinder its flow. This chapter offers practical advice and recipes that align with the principles of spiritual nutrition, emphasizing the importance of a clean and balanced diet in sustaining Kundalini activation. Visualize yourself preparing meals that are not only healthy but also infused with spiritual intent, each bite bringing you closer to your divine nature.

The fifth pillar, Sound and Mantras, immerses you in the transformative power of sound. Through the practice of chanting ancient mantras, you will experience how sound vibrations can cleanse and elevate your energetic state, aiding in the awakening process. This chapter introduces various mantras and explains their significance, providing you with powerful tools to enhance your spiritual practice.

Visualization and Intention Setting, the sixth pillar, harnesses the creative power of your mind. Guided visualizations and intention-setting exercises will help you manifest your spiritual goals and draw closer to the divine. This chapter teaches you how to create a vivid and compelling vision of your aspirations, each intention a seed planted in the fertile ground of your consciousness, destined to grow and flourish.

Finally, the seventh pillar, Community and Support, underscores the importance of finding and nurturing a spiritual community. No journey is meant to be undertaken alone, and having a support system can amplify your efforts and provide much-needed encouragement. This chapter guides you on how to connect with like-minded individuals, fostering a sense of belonging and collective growth. Imagine being surrounded by a network of light, each person contributing to the collective energy, elevating everyone involved.

Through these seven pillars, "Divine Energy: Seven Pillars for Spiritual Awakening and Kundalini Activation" aims to provide a comprehensive and accessible guide to your spiritual journey. It seeks to inspire and empower you, offering practical tools and timeless wisdom to awaken the divine energy within. As you delve into these teachings, you will not only transform your own life but also contribute to the collective awakening of humanity, stepping into your true power as a radiant being of light.

Understanding Divine Energy

In the boundless expanse of the universe, a profound and mystical force permeates all that exists. This force, often referred to as divine energy, is the very essence of life, the invisible thread that weaves through the fabric of our existence. Understanding and harnessing this divine energy is not merely an esoteric pursuit; it is a journey towards enlightenment, a path to realizing our true potential, and a means to attain profound inner peace and harmony.

Imagine for a moment standing on the edge of a vast ocean, feeling the rhythmic pulse of the waves beneath your feet, the gentle caress of the breeze, and the infinite horizon stretching before you. This ocean is a metaphor for divine energy – ever-present, boundless, and deeply interconnected with every aspect of life. Just as the ocean's currents shape the landscape, divine energy flows through us, influencing our thoughts, emotions, and actions. To truly understand and harness this energy is to align ourselves with the very heartbeat of the cosmos.

The first step in this sacred journey is the recognition that divine energy resides within each of us. It is the spark that animates our being, the force that drives our desires, and the light that guides our spiritual path. This energy, often symbolized by the coiled serpent known as Kundalini, lies dormant at the base of our spine, waiting to be awakened. When we embark on the path of awakening this energy, we open ourselves to a transformative experience that transcends the ordinary and connects us to the divine.

Harnessing divine energy involves cultivating a deep awareness of its presence and learning to channel it effectively. This requires a harmonious integration of body, mind, and spirit. Through practices such as meditation, breathwork, and yoga, we can learn to tap into this energy, directing it to flow through our chakras, the energy centers within our bodies. Each chakra corresponds to different aspects of our physical, emotional, and spiritual well-being. By awakening and balancing these chakras, we create a clear pathway for divine energy to rise, leading to a state of heightened consciousness and spiritual awakening.

Meditation serves as a powerful tool in this process. By stilling the mind and turning our focus inward, we create a sacred space where divine energy can be felt and nurtured. Imagine sitting in quiet meditation, the world around you fading into silence, and within that silence, a gentle warmth begins to rise from the base of your spine. This warmth is the awakening of your Kundalini energy, a reminder of your inherent connection to the divine. Regular meditation practice not only awakens this energy but also helps in maintaining its flow, ensuring that it nourishes every aspect of your being.

Breathwork, or pranayama, is another essential practice for harnessing divine energy. The breath is the bridge between the body and the spirit, a conduit for life force energy, or prana. Through conscious and controlled breathing techniques, we can invigorate our energy centers and facilitate the smooth ascent of Kundalini. Picture yourself engaging in deep, rhythmic breathing, each inhale drawing in the life force of the universe, and each exhale releasing tension and negativity. This practice not only revitalizes the body but also purifies the mind, making it a fertile ground for spiritual growth.

Physical movement, particularly through the practice of yoga asanas, plays a crucial role in awakening and channeling divine energy. Yoga postures are designed to align the body, open the chakras, and create a free flow of energy. As you move through a series of asanas, imagine each posture as a key that unlocks the potential of your energy centers, allowing divine energy to flow unhindered. This movement not only strengthens the body but also harmonizes it with the rhythm of the universe, creating a perfect vessel for the divine.

Understanding and harnessing divine energy also involves nurturing our physical bodies with the right nutrition. The foods we consume can either enhance our energy flow or create blockages. By adopting a diet rich in prana, or life force, we provide our bodies with the sustenance needed to support our spiritual practices. Think of each meal as an offering to the divine within you, each bite nourishing your body and elevating your spirit. Foods that are fresh, vibrant, and pure carry high levels of prana and are essential for maintaining the flow of divine energy.

Sound and mantras are powerful tools for awakening and channeling divine energy. The vibrations created by chanting mantras resonate with our energy centers, breaking down barriers and facilitating the rise of Kundalini. Envision yourself chanting a sacred mantra, each syllable vibrating through your being, dissolving negativity and creating a resonance with the divine. This practice not only awakens your energy but also attunes you to the higher frequencies of the universe, enhancing your connection to the divine.

Visualization and intention setting are integral to harnessing divine energy. The mind is a powerful tool, and when used correctly, it can manifest our deepest spiritual aspirations. Through guided visualizations, we can create a vivid and compelling vision of our spiritual journey, setting clear intentions that direct our energy towards our goals. Imagine yourself visualizing a radiant light rising from the base of your spine, illuminating each chakra as it ascends, and setting an intention to awaken your Kundalini. This mental focus not only guides your energy but also aligns your actions with your spiritual purpose.

Finally, the importance of community and support cannot be overstated. The journey of awakening and harnessing divine energy is profound and often challenging. Surrounding yourself with like-minded individuals who share your spiritual goals can provide invaluable support and encouragement. Imagine being part of a community where each member's energy contributes to a collective light, amplifying your own efforts and creating a powerful network of spiritual growth. This sense of belonging and shared purpose can significantly enhance your journey, providing the strength and inspiration needed to continue on your path.

In essence, understanding and harnessing divine energy is about aligning ourselves with the fundamental forces of the universe. It is a journey that transforms every aspect of our being, leading to a state of enlightenment and profound inner peace. As you delve into the teachings of "Divine Energy: Seven Pillars for Spiritual Awakening and Kundalini Activation," you will not only awaken your own divine energy but also contribute to the collective awakening of humanity. This journey is not just about personal growth; it is about becoming a beacon of light in the world, radiating divine energy and inspiring others to embark on their own spiritual paths. Embrace this journey with an open heart and a willing spirit, and let the divine energy within you shine brightly, illuminating the path to a higher consciousness and a deeper connection with the universe.

In the mystical dance of existence, where the seen and unseen merge, lie the seven foundational principles that will guide you through the awakening of your divine energy and the activation of your Kundalini. These seven pillars are the bedrock of this journey, each one a vital element that harmonizes and enhances your spiritual practice. As you embark on this sacred path, these pillars will serve as your compass, guiding you through the intricate labyrinth of your inner world, unlocking the boundless potential within.

The first pillar, Meditation and Mindfulness, is the gateway to the divine. Meditation is not merely a practice but a state of being, a profound stillness where the soul finds its true voice. In this chapter, you will learn to quiet the incessant chatter of the mind and immerse yourself in the serene depths of inner silence. Through detailed descriptions and practical exercises, you will discover how regular meditation can elevate your consciousness, allowing you to connect with the divine source. Mindfulness, the art of being fully present, complements meditation by grounding you in the here and now, making every moment a sacred experience.

Breathwork and Pranayama, the second pillar, explores the sacred art of controlling the breath, the life force that animates all beings. The breath is a bridge between the physical and the spiritual, a conduit through which divine energy flows. In this chapter, you will delve into various pranayama techniques, each one designed to purify and invigorate your energy centers.

Imagine each breath as a thread connecting you to the cosmos, drawing in the universal life force with each inhale and releasing toxins and negativity with each exhale. This practice not only revitalizes the body but also prepares it for the rise of Kundalini, creating a harmonious flow of energy.

The third pillar, Physical Asanas and Movement, emphasizes the importance of aligning the body to support the awakening of divine energy. Yoga asanas are more than physical postures; they are spiritual tools that open and balance the chakras, creating a clear pathway for energy to ascend. In this chapter, you will learn specific Kundalini yoga poses that strengthen and purify the body, making it a fit vessel for divine energy. Visualize each movement as a sacred dance, a harmonious alignment of body, mind, and spirit that prepares you for the transformative journey ahead.

Diet and Nutrition, the fourth pillar, explores the profound connection between what you consume and your spiritual well-being. The food you eat can either enhance your energy flow or create blockages. This chapter will guide you through the principles of spiritual nutrition, offering practical advice and recipes that nourish both body and soul. Imagine each meal as an offering to the divine within you, each bite infused with the intention of supporting your spiritual journey. By adopting a diet rich in prana, or life force, you create a foundation for a healthy and vibrant energy flow, essential for sustaining Kundalini activation.

The fifth pillar, Sound and Mantras, immerses you in the transformative power of sound. The vibrations created by chanting mantras resonate with your energy centers, breaking down barriers and facilitating the rise of Kundalini. In this chapter, you will explore the ancient practice of using sound as a tool for healing and spiritual growth. Picture yourself chanting sacred mantras, each syllable vibrating through your being, dissolving negativity and elevating your consciousness. This practice not only awakens your energy but also attunes you to the higher frequencies of the universe, enhancing your connection to the divine.

Visualization and Intention Setting, the sixth pillar, harnesses the power of your mind to manifest your spiritual goals. Through guided visualizations and intention-setting exercises, you will learn to create a vivid and compelling vision of your spiritual aspirations. This chapter will teach you how to focus your mental energy, setting clear and powerful intentions that direct your actions and align you with your higher purpose. Imagine visualizing a radiant light rising from the base of your spine, illuminating each chakra as it ascends, each intention a seed planted in the fertile ground of your consciousness, destined to bloom into reality.

Finally, the seventh pillar, Community and Support, underscores the importance of finding and nurturing a spiritual community. No journey is meant to be undertaken alone, and having a support system can amplify your efforts and provide much-needed encouragement. This chapter will guide you on how to connect with like-minded individuals who share your spiritual goals, creating a network of light that elevates everyone involved. Imagine being surrounded by a community where each member's energy contributes to a collective light, fostering a sense of belonging and shared purpose that significantly enhances your spiritual journey.

Through these seven pillars, "Divine Energy: Seven Pillars for Spiritual Awakening and Kundalini Activation" provides a comprehensive and accessible guide to your spiritual journey. It seeks to inspire and empower you, offering practical tools and timeless wisdom to awaken the divine energy within. As you delve into these teachings, you will not only transform your own life but also contribute to the collective awakening of humanity, stepping into your true power as a radiant being of light. This journey is not just about personal growth; it is about becoming a beacon of light in the world, radiating divine energy and inspiring others to embark on their own spiritual paths. Embrace this journey with an open heart and a willing spirit, and let the divine energy within you shine brightly, illuminating the path to a higher consciousness and a deeper connection with the universe.

Harnessing Divine Energy

In the intricate dance of the cosmos, an unseen force weaves through the fabric of existence, binding everything in a harmonious symphony of life. This force, often referred to as divine energy, is the essence of all creation, the primal power that fuels our spirit and connects us to the universe. To understand and harness this divine energy is to embark on a journey of expanded awareness and profound knowledge, a journey that transforms not only our inner world but also our interaction with the world around us.

Divine energy is not a concept confined to the abstract; it is a tangible presence that can be felt, nurtured, and directed. This energy resides within us all, coiled like a serpent at the base of our spine, waiting to be awakened. This dormant energy, known as Kundalini, represents the unmanifested potential within us, the divine spark that, when ignited, illuminates our consciousness and elevates our existence. Understanding this energy begins with recognizing its presence and acknowledging its profound impact on our physical, emotional, and spiritual well-being.

Imagine, if you will, standing on the precipice of a vast ocean, feeling the rhythmic pulse of the waves beneath your feet, the gentle caress of the breeze, and the infinite horizon stretching before you. This ocean is a metaphor for divine energy – ever-present, boundless, and deeply interconnected with every aspect of life. Just as the ocean's currents shape the landscape, divine energy flows through us, influencing our thoughts, emotions, and actions. By becoming aware of this energy, we open ourselves to a deeper understanding of our true nature and our place in the universe.

Expanded awareness is the first step in harnessing divine energy. This awareness is cultivated through practices that quiet the mind and open the heart, allowing us to perceive the subtle energies that permeate our being. Meditation, for example, is a powerful tool for expanding awareness. By stilling the mind and turning our focus inward, we create a space where the whispers of the divine can be heard. Imagine sitting in quiet meditation, the world around you fading into silence, and within that silence, a gentle warmth begins to rise from the base of your spine. This warmth is the awakening of your Kundalini energy, a reminder of your inherent connection to the divine.

Breathwork, or pranayama, is another essential practice for understanding and harnessing divine energy. The breath is the bridge between the body and the spirit, a conduit for life force energy, or prana. Through conscious and controlled breathing techniques, we can invigorate our energy centers and facilitate the smooth ascent of Kundalini. Picture yourself engaging in deep, rhythmic breathing, each inhale drawing in the life force of the universe, and each exhale releasing tension and negativity. This practice not only revitalizes the body but also purifies the mind, making it a fertile ground for spiritual growth.

As we deepen our understanding of divine energy, we begin to realize that it is not limited to our physical being but extends into the very fabric of the cosmos. This realization leads to an expanded knowledge of the interconnectedness of all life. Everything in the universe, from the smallest atom to the vast galaxies, is imbued with divine energy. By tuning into this energy, we can tap into a universal wisdom that transcends time and space. This wisdom reveals itself in moments of profound clarity and insight, guiding us on our spiritual path.

One profound way to experience this expanded knowledge is through the practice of visualization and intention setting. Visualization harnesses the creative power of the mind to manifest our spiritual goals. Through guided visualizations, we can create a vivid and compelling vision of our spiritual aspirations. Imagine visualizing a radiant light rising from the base of your spine, illuminating each chakra as it ascends, each intention a seed planted in the fertile ground of your consciousness, destined to grow and flourish. This mental focus not only guides your energy but also aligns your actions with your spiritual purpose.

Another key aspect of understanding and harnessing divine energy is the recognition of its presence in the natural world. Nature is a powerful reflection of divine energy, with its rhythms and cycles mirroring the flow of energy within us. Spending time in nature, whether through a walk in the forest, a swim in the ocean, or simply sitting in a garden, can attune us to the natural flow of energy and deepen our connection to the divine. Imagine standing beneath a towering tree, feeling the strength and stability of its roots, the graceful sway of its branches, and the vibrant life coursing through its veins. This connection to nature reminds us of our own vitality and the divine energy that sustains us.

The final element in harnessing divine energy is the cultivation of a supportive community. The journey of awakening and understanding divine energy is profound and often challenging. Surrounding yourself with like-minded individuals who share your spiritual goals can provide invaluable support and encouragement. Imagine being part of a community where each member's energy contributes to a collective light, amplifying your own efforts and creating a powerful network of spiritual growth. This sense of belonging and shared purpose can significantly enhance your journey, providing the strength and inspiration needed to continue on your path.

In essence, understanding and harnessing divine energy is about aligning ourselves with the fundamental forces of the universe. It is a journey that transforms every aspect of our being, leading to a state of enlightenment and profound inner peace. As you delve into the teachings of "Divine Energy: Seven Pillars for Spiritual Awakening and Kundalini Activation," you will not only awaken your own divine energy but also contribute to the collective awakening of humanity. This journey is not just about personal growth; it is about becoming a beacon of light in the world, radiating divine energy and inspiring others to embark on their own spiritual paths. Embrace this journey with an open heart and a willing spirit, and let the divine energy within you shine brightly, illuminating the path to a higher consciousness and a deeper connection with the universe.

In the vast expanse of the cosmos, there exists a force so profound and all-encompassing that it defies simple explanation. This force, often referred to as divine energy, is the essence of life itself, the vital spark that animates all beings and binds the universe together in a harmonious dance of existence. To define and understand divine energy is to glimpse the very heart of creation, to touch the sacred and the eternal within ourselves and the world around us.

Divine energy is the primordial force from which all life springs. It is the breath of the cosmos, the invisible current that flows through every atom, every star, and every living being. This energy is known by many names across different cultures and spiritual traditions. In Hindu philosophy, it is called Prana, the life force that pervades the universe. In Chinese tradition, it is Qi, the vital energy that sustains life. In ancient Egyptian texts, it is referred to as Ka, the spiritual essence that inhabits all living things. Despite the varied nomenclature, the essence remains the same—a sacred energy that connects all existence.

The significance of divine energy lies in its ability to transform and elevate the human experience. At the core of our being, this energy lies dormant, like a coiled serpent, known as Kundalini in yogic traditions. When awakened, Kundalini rises through the chakras, the energy centers within our bodies, bringing about a profound spiritual awakening and heightened awareness. This awakening is not merely a metaphysical phenomenon but a deeply transformative process that impacts every aspect of our existence.

To illustrate, imagine a seed buried deep within the earth. This seed holds within it the potential for a magnificent tree, but it requires the right conditions to awaken and grow. Similarly, the Kundalini energy within us holds the potential for spiritual enlightenment and personal transformation. Through practices such as meditation, breathwork, and yoga, we create the conditions for this energy to rise, nurturing it as it ascends through the chakras, each step bringing us closer to our true nature and divine purpose.

The journey of awakening this divine energy is akin to embarking on a sacred pilgrimage. It requires dedication, discipline, and an open heart. Meditation serves as a crucial tool in this journey, allowing us to quiet the mind and attune ourselves to the subtle vibrations of divine energy. Picture yourself in a serene space, free from distractions, your breath steady and calm. As you meditate, a gentle warmth begins to rise from the base of your spine, a sign of the awakening Kundalini. This warmth spreads through your body, illuminating your chakras, and filling you with a sense of peace and connection to the divine.

Breathwork, or Pranayama, further amplifies this connection. By controlling our breath, we regulate the flow of prana within us, balancing our energy and enhancing our awareness. Imagine practicing deep, rhythmic breathing, each inhale drawing in the life force of the universe, and each exhale releasing tension and negativity. This conscious control of breath not only invigorates the body but also purifies the mind, creating a fertile ground for the awakening of divine energy.

The physical practice of Yoga Asanas also plays a vital role in harnessing divine energy. These postures are designed to align the body and open the chakras, facilitating the free flow of energy. Visualize moving through a series of yoga poses, each one a step in a sacred dance, harmonizing body, mind, and spirit. As you flow from one pose to another, you become a vessel for divine energy, allowing it to rise and illuminate your being.

Understanding and harnessing divine energy also involves recognizing its presence in the natural world. Nature, in all its beauty and majesty, is a reflection of divine energy. Consider the cycles of the moon, the rhythm of the tides, and the changing seasons—each is a manifestation of this sacred energy. By attuning ourselves to these natural rhythms, we deepen our connection to the divine. Imagine standing in a forest, the trees towering above you, their leaves rustling in the wind. The air is filled with the scent of earth and foliage, and the ground beneath your feet pulses with life. In this moment, you feel a profound connection to the natural world and the divine energy that sustains it.

The significance of divine energy extends beyond personal transformation. It is a unifying force that connects us to all of creation. By awakening and harnessing this energy, we align ourselves with the greater flow of the universe, transcending the limitations of the physical world and entering a state of higher consciousness. This expanded awareness brings a deep sense of peace and fulfillment, a recognition of our place in the cosmic order, and a profound sense of interconnectedness with all life.

In essence, divine energy is the essence of who we are. It is the light that guides us, the force that empowers us, and the sacred thread that weaves us into the tapestry of existence. As you journey through the teachings of "Divine Energy: Seven Pillars for Spiritual Awakening and Kundalini Activation," you will not only awaken this energy within yourself but also contribute to the collective awakening of humanity. Embrace this journey with an open heart and a willing spirit, and let the divine energy within you shine brightly, illuminating the path to a higher consciousness and a deeper connection with the universe.

In the grand tapestry of the cosmos, an invisible yet omnipresent force interweaves through every strand, binding all of creation in a harmonious symphony of existence. This force, known as divine energy, is the essence of life itself. It is the primordial current that flows through the universe, animating every being, nurturing every star, and infusing the cosmos with vitality and purpose. To understand what divine energy is, one must transcend the boundaries of the physical world and venture into the mystical realms where the seen and unseen converge.

Divine energy, often referred to by various names across different spiritual traditions, is the lifeblood of the universe. In Hindu philosophy, it is known as Prana, the vital life force that sustains all living things. In Chinese tradition, it is called Qi, the energy that flows through the meridians, sustaining life and promoting balance. In ancient Egyptian belief, it is referred to as Ka, the spiritual essence that resides within every being. Despite the differences in terminology, the concept remains consistent: divine energy is the fundamental force that connects and animates all aspects of existence.

Imagine, if you will, a vast ocean that stretches infinitely in all directions. This ocean is a metaphor for divine energy—boundless, omnipresent, and ever-flowing. Just as the ocean's waves touch every shore, divine energy permeates every corner of the universe, from the smallest particle to the largest galaxy. It is the force that breathes life into the inanimate, the spark that ignites the soul, and the rhythm that orchestrates the dance of the cosmos.

At the core of our being, this divine energy resides in a dormant state, coiled like a serpent at the base of our spine. This energy, known as Kundalini in yogic traditions, holds the key to our spiritual awakening and transformation. When awakened, Kundalini rises through the chakras, the energy centers within our bodies, purifying and illuminating them, and leading us to a state of heightened consciousness and profound enlightenment. This journey of awakening is not merely a metaphysical concept but a deeply transformative process that impacts every facet of our existence.

To illustrate, consider the metaphor of a seed buried deep within the earth. This seed, though seemingly inert, holds within it the potential for a magnificent tree. However, it requires the right conditions—nourishment, light, and water—to awaken and grow. Similarly, the Kundalini energy within us holds the potential for spiritual enlightenment and personal transformation. Through practices such as meditation, breathwork, and yoga, we create the conditions for this energy to awaken, nurturing it as it ascends through the chakras, each step bringing us closer to our true nature and divine purpose.

Meditation serves as a powerful tool in this awakening process. By quieting the mind and turning our focus inward, we create a space where the subtle vibrations of divine energy can be felt and nurtured. Imagine sitting in serene meditation, the chaos of the outside world fading into silence. In this stillness, a gentle warmth begins to rise from the base of your spine, spreading through your body, illuminating your chakras, and filling you with a sense of peace and connection to the divine. This warmth is the awakening of your Kundalini energy, a reminder of your inherent connection to the divine source.

Breathwork, or pranayama, further amplifies this connection. The breath is the bridge between the physical and the spiritual, a conduit for life force energy. Through conscious and controlled breathing techniques, we invigorate our energy centers and facilitate the smooth ascent of Kundalini. Picture yourself engaging in deep, rhythmic breathing, each inhale drawing in the life force of the universe, and each exhale releasing tension and negativity. This practice not only revitalizes the body but also purifies the mind, creating a fertile ground for the awakening of divine energy.

The physical practice of yoga asanas also plays a crucial role in harnessing divine energy. These postures are designed to align the body and open the chakras, facilitating the free flow of energy. Visualize moving through a series of yoga poses, each one a step in a sacred dance, harmonizing body, mind, and spirit. As you flow from one pose to another, you become a vessel for divine energy, allowing it to rise and illuminate your being.

Divine energy is also intricately connected to the natural world. Nature, in all its beauty and majesty, is a reflection of this sacred energy. Consider the cycles of the moon, the rhythm of the tides, and the changing seasons—each is a manifestation of divine energy. By attuning ourselves to these natural rhythms, we deepen our connection to the divine. Imagine standing in a forest, the trees towering above you, their leaves rustling in the wind. The air is filled with the scent of earth and foliage, and the ground beneath your feet pulses with life. In this moment, you feel a profound connection to the natural world and the divine energy that sustains it.

Understanding and harnessing divine energy also involves recognizing its presence in our daily lives. This energy is not confined to moments of meditation or spiritual practice but is present in every breath, every heartbeat, and every thought. By cultivating awareness and mindfulness, we can tune into this energy, allowing it to guide and inspire us. Imagine approaching each day with a sense of reverence and gratitude, recognizing the divine energy that flows through you and around you. This awareness transforms ordinary moments into sacred experiences, infusing your life with a sense of purpose and meaning.

In essence, divine energy is the essence of who we are. It is the light that guides us, the force that empowers us, and the sacred thread that weaves us into the tapestry of existence. As you journey through the teachings of "Divine Energy: Seven Pillars for Spiritual Awakening and Kundalini Activation," you will not only awaken this energy within yourself but also contribute to the collective awakening of humanity. Embrace this journey with an open heart and a willing spirit, and let the divine energy within you shine brightly, illuminating the path to a higher consciousness and a deeper connection with the universe.

In the vast, intricate tapestry of the universe, a subtle yet powerful force lies dormant within each of us, waiting to be awakened. This force, known as Kundalini energy, is the essence of divine power, the primal energy that fuels our spiritual journey and leads us towards enlightenment. Understanding Kundalini energy and its role in spiritual awakening is to glimpse the profound potential that resides within us, a potential that, when realized, transforms our lives and connects us to the divine.

Kundalini energy is often depicted as a coiled serpent resting at the base of the spine, symbolizing the latent spiritual power that lies within. This imagery is not merely metaphorical; it reflects the deep, transformative nature of this energy. In its dormant state, Kundalini energy is a reservoir of untapped potential, holding the keys to higher consciousness, profound wisdom, and spiritual liberation. The journey of awakening this energy is akin to embarking on a sacred quest, one that requires dedication, discipline, and an open heart.

The process of Kundalini awakening begins with the recognition of its presence within us. This energy, known by various names across different spiritual traditions, is the life force that sustains all living beings. In Hindu philosophy, it is called Prana; in Chinese tradition, it is known as Qi; and in ancient Egyptian belief, it is referred to as Sekhem. Despite the differences in terminology, the concept remains the same: Kundalini energy is the divine spark that animates our being, the bridge between the physical and the spiritual.

To awaken Kundalini energy is to initiate a profound transformation, a journey that takes us through the seven chakras, or energy centers, within our bodies. Each chakra represents a different aspect of our being, from the physical to the spiritual. The awakening of Kundalini energy involves guiding this force through these chakras, purifying and illuminating them, and ultimately achieving a state of spiritual enlightenment.

The first chakra, known as the Muladhara or Root Chakra, is located at the base of the spine and is associated with our basic survival instincts and physical identity. When Kundalini energy begins to rise, it activates this chakra, grounding us and providing the stability needed for our spiritual journey. As the energy ascends, it moves to the Swadhisthana or Sacral Chakra, located in the lower abdomen, which governs our creativity, emotions, and sexual energy. The activation of this chakra unleashes our creative potential and emotional balance, paving the way for further spiritual growth.

The journey continues to the Manipura or Solar Plexus Chakra, situated just above the navel, which is the center of our personal power and self-esteem. The rising Kundalini energy empowers us, instilling confidence and the strength to overcome obstacles. As the energy flows upward, it reaches the Anahata or Heart Chakra, located at the center of the chest. This chakra is the seat of love, compassion, and connection, and its activation opens our hearts to unconditional love and divine compassion.

The next stage of the journey involves the Vishuddha or Throat Chakra, located at the throat, which governs communication and self-expression. When Kundalini energy activates this chakra, it enhances our ability to express our truth and connect with others on a deeper level. The energy then ascends to the Ajna or Third Eye Chakra, located between the eyebrows, which is the center of intuition and spiritual insight. The activation of this chakra opens our inner vision, allowing us to perceive the subtle realms and gain profound spiritual insights.

Finally, the journey culminates at the Sahasrara or Crown Chakra, located at the top of the head. This chakra represents our connection to the divine and the infinite. When Kundalini energy fully awakens and reaches this chakra, it unites us with the divine consciousness, leading to a state of spiritual enlightenment and bliss. This union, known as Samadhi in yogic tradition, is the ultimate goal of the Kundalini awakening process.

The awakening of Kundalini energy is not a mere theoretical concept but a deeply transformative experience that has been documented and revered by mystics, sages, and spiritual practitioners throughout history. One of the most notable examples is Sri Ramakrishna, a 19th-century Indian mystic, whose intense spiritual practices and devotion led to the spontaneous awakening of his Kundalini energy. Ramakrishna's experiences of divine ecstasy and profound spiritual insights are well-documented, serving as a testament to the transformative power of Kundalini awakening.

Another significant figure is Gopi Krishna, a 20th-century Indian spiritual teacher, whose detailed accounts of his Kundalini awakening provide valuable insights into the process. Gopi Krishna described his experience as a powerful surge of energy rising from the base of his spine, leading to profound changes in his consciousness and perception of reality. His writings emphasize the importance of preparation, discipline, and guidance in navigating the Kundalini awakening process.

The role of Kundalini energy in spiritual awakening extends beyond personal transformation. It is a journey that connects us to the universal life force, transcending the limitations of the physical world and opening us to the infinite possibilities of the divine. As Kundalini energy rises and activates the chakras, it purifies and transforms our being, leading to a state of higher consciousness and spiritual enlightenment.

In essence, Kundalini energy is the essence of who we are. It is the divine spark that fuels our spiritual journey, the bridge between the physical and the spiritual, and the key to unlocking our true potential. As you journey through the teachings of "Divine Energy: Seven Pillars for Spiritual Awakening and Kundalini Activation," you will not only awaken this energy within yourself but also contribute to the collective awakening of humanity. Embrace this journey with an open heart and a willing spirit, and let the divine energy within you rise, illuminating your path to higher consciousness and deeper connection with the universe.

In the rich tapestry of spiritual symbolism, few images are as evocative and profound as the coiled serpent. This ancient symbol, found across numerous cultures and spiritual traditions, represents the latent divine energy within every individual. Known as Kundalini in yogic philosophy, the coiled serpent signifies potential, transformation, and the journey towards enlightenment. Understanding the symbolism of the coiled serpent can inspire us to awaken this dormant energy and embark on a path of spiritual awakening.

The image of the serpent coiled at the base of the spine is deeply rooted in the ancient traditions of India. In Sanskrit, the term "Kundalini" derives from "kundal," meaning coiled or spiral. This powerful metaphor depicts the dormant energy that lies within us, waiting to be awakened and directed through the chakras, or energy centers, of the body. The serpent's coiled form suggests both potential energy and a state of readiness, akin to a spring compressed and poised to release its force.

The symbolism of the serpent is multifaceted and rich with meaning. At its core, the serpent represents the cyclical nature of life, death, and rebirth. In many cultures, serpents are seen as guardians of sacred knowledge and gateways to higher realms of consciousness. This dual nature of the serpent—as both protector and transformer—reflects the journey of Kundalini awakening, where one must navigate the challenges of personal transformation to access deeper spiritual truths.

In Hindu mythology, the serpent is often associated with the god Shiva, the deity of destruction and regeneration. The imagery of Shiva meditating with a coiled serpent around his neck embodies the control and mastery over Kundalini energy. This powerful symbol teaches that through disciplined practice and inner focus, one can harness this energy for spiritual growth and transformation.

The coiled serpent also appears prominently in other spiritual traditions. In ancient Egyptian mythology, the serpent represents the primal life force and divine wisdom. The Uraeus, a symbol of a rearing cobra worn by pharaohs, signifies the awakened Kundalini energy and the ruler's connection to divine power. This imagery underscores the transformative potential of Kundalini, capable of elevating an individual to a state of higher consciousness and divine authority.

In the Greco-Roman tradition, the caduceus—a staff entwined by two serpents—symbolizes healing and spiritual awakening. The intertwining serpents represent the duality of existence and the balance between opposing forces. This symbol aligns with the journey of Kundalini energy as it rises through the chakras, harmonizing the body, mind, and spirit. The caduceus thus becomes a powerful emblem of the healing and unifying potential of awakened Kundalini energy.

The symbolism of the coiled serpent extends beyond historical and cultural contexts, offering profound insights into the nature of spiritual awakening. The serpent's coiled position at the base of the spine signifies the potential for profound transformation within each of us. Just as a serpent sheds its skin, the process of Kundalini awakening involves shedding old patterns and limitations, allowing for spiritual rebirth and renewal.

The journey of the coiled serpent through the chakras mirrors the path of spiritual ascent. As Kundalini energy rises from the base of the spine to the crown of the head, it activates and purifies each chakra, leading to expanded awareness and heightened states of consciousness. This journey is not linear but cyclical, reflecting the ongoing process of growth, transformation, and integration. The serpent's movement symbolizes the dynamic and evolving nature of spiritual awakening, where each stage of the journey brings deeper insights and greater alignment with the divine.

In personal spiritual practice, the imagery of the coiled serpent can serve as a powerful catalyst for transformation. Meditating on the serpent at the base of the spine can help focus one's intention on awakening and directing Kundalini energy. Visualizing the serpent's ascent through the chakras can enhance the flow of energy and support the process of spiritual awakening. This practice aligns with the ancient teachings of Kundalini yoga, which combine breathwork, movement, and meditation to awaken and harness this powerful energy.

The symbolism of the coiled serpent also teaches the importance of patience and readiness in the journey of spiritual awakening. Just as a serpent waits patiently in its coiled state, so too must we cultivate patience and readiness for the transformative process of Kundalini awakening. This involves preparing the mind, body, and spirit through disciplined practice, creating a conducive environment for the energy to rise and flow freely.

Ultimately, the coiled serpent symbolizes the profound potential within each of us to awaken to our true nature and realize our divine essence. It is a reminder that the journey of spiritual awakening is not a destination but an ongoing process of growth, transformation, and integration. As we navigate this journey, the symbolism of the serpent inspires us to embrace our potential, overcome our limitations, and align with the divine energy that flows through all of creation.

In essence, the coiled serpent is a powerful symbol of the dormant divine energy within us, the potential for profound transformation, and the journey towards spiritual enlightenment. As you delve into the teachings of "Divine Energy: Seven Pillars for Spiritual Awakening and Kundalini Activation," let the symbolism of the coiled serpent inspire you to awaken this energy within yourself. Embrace the journey with an open heart and a willing spirit, and let the serpent's ascent illuminate your path to higher consciousness and deeper connection with the universe.

In the grand tapestry of human history, the concept of divine energy has woven itself through the spiritual and cultural practices of civilizations across the globe. One of the most profound manifestations of this concept is Kundalini energy, a force that has been revered, studied, and sought after by mystics, sages, and spiritual seekers for millennia. To delve into the historical and cultural perspectives on Kundalini energy is to embark on a journey through the annals of time, exploring the rich tapestry of beliefs and practices that have shaped our understanding of this mystical force.

The origins of Kundalini energy can be traced back to ancient India, where it is deeply rooted in the spiritual traditions of Hinduism and Tantra. The term "Kundalini" itself comes from the Sanskrit word "kundal," meaning coiled or spiral. This is a reference to the coiled serpent said to reside at the base of the spine, a powerful metaphor for the latent divine energy within every individual. The earliest references to Kundalini energy appear in the Upanishads, ancient Indian texts that form the philosophical foundation of Hinduism. These texts describe Kundalini as a dormant energy coiled like a serpent at the base of the spine, which, when awakened, rises through the chakras, or energy centers, leading to spiritual enlightenment and union with the divine.

One of the most notable figures in the history of Kundalini energy is Patanjali, the sage who codified the practice of yoga in his seminal work, the Yoga Sutras. Patanjali's teachings emphasize the importance of purifying the mind and body through disciplined practice, preparing the practitioner for the awakening of Kundalini. His work laid the groundwork for the systematic study and practice of yoga, which continues to be a vital aspect of Kundalini awakening.

The Tantric tradition further elaborates on the concept of Kundalini energy, presenting it as a fundamental aspect of spiritual practice. Tantra, which emerged around the 6th century CE, offers a rich and intricate system of rituals, meditations, and esoteric practices designed to awaken and harness this divine energy. The Tantric texts, known as Agamas and Nigamas, provide detailed instructions on how to awaken Kundalini and guide it through the chakras, ultimately achieving a state of spiritual liberation known as moksha. This journey of Kundalini is often depicted in Tantric iconography, with elaborate representations of the chakras and the nadis (energy channels) through which the energy flows.

Moving forward in history, the influence of Kundalini energy can be seen in the teachings of Swami Vivekananda, a key figure in the introduction of Indian spiritual practices to the Western world in the late 19th and early 20th centuries. Vivekananda's lectures and writings emphasized the transformative power of Kundalini energy, describing it as the key to unlocking one's spiritual potential. He encouraged practitioners to engage in disciplined yoga practices to awaken this energy, thus bridging the gap between Eastern and Western spiritual traditions.

In the 20th century, the study and practice of Kundalini energy gained further prominence through the work of Carl Jung, the Swiss psychologist and founder of analytical psychology. Jung's exploration of Kundalini was part of his broader interest in the intersection of psychology and spirituality. He viewed Kundalini awakening as a profound process of individuation, where the individual integrates the conscious and unconscious aspects of the self, leading to psychological wholeness and spiritual enlightenment. Jung's seminar on Kundalini yoga in 1932 remains a seminal work, offering a psychological perspective on this ancient spiritual practice.

The cultural impact of Kundalini energy extends beyond India and the West. In Tibet, the practice of Kundalini yoga is intertwined with the Vajrayana Buddhist tradition. Tibetan Buddhists refer to this energy as Tummo, the inner fire, which is cultivated through advanced meditative practices to achieve spiritual awakening and physical vitality. The teachings of Milarepa, one of Tibet's most revered yogis, emphasize the importance of awakening Tummo to attain enlightenment.

Kundalini energy also finds parallels in other cultures and spiritual traditions. In China, the concept of Qi bears a striking resemblance to Kundalini. Traditional Chinese Medicine and practices such as Qigong and Tai Chi focus on cultivating and balancing Qi to promote health and spiritual well-being. The ancient Egyptians, too, had a concept of divine energy, known as Sekhem, which was integral to their spiritual and healing practices.

Understanding the historical and cultural perspectives on Kundalini energy illuminates its universal significance and timeless appeal. This energy, though described differently across cultures, represents a common quest for spiritual awakening and connection with the divine. It is a testament to the shared human experience of seeking something greater, something that transcends the material world and touches the sacred.

In contemporary times, the practice of Kundalini yoga has continued to evolve and spread globally, thanks to the efforts of teachers like Yogi Bhajan, who introduced Kundalini yoga to the West in the late 1960s. Yogi Bhajan's teachings emphasize the integration of physical, mental, and spiritual practices to awaken Kundalini energy, offering a comprehensive approach that is accessible to modern practitioners.

As you journey through the teachings of "Divine Energy: Seven Pillars for Spiritual Awakening and Kundalini Activation," you will not only explore the rich historical and cultural context of Kundalini energy but also engage with practical techniques to awaken and harness this divine force within yourself. This journey is a continuation of a timeless tradition, a path walked by countless seekers before you, each one contributing to the collective understanding and evolution of this sacred practice.

Embrace this journey with an open heart and a willing spirit, and let the wisdom of the ages guide you. Allow the divine energy within you to awaken, rise, and illuminate your path, leading you to a state of higher consciousness and deeper connection with the universe. In doing so, you become a part of this ancient and ever-evolving tradition, a beacon of light and inspiration for future generations of seekers.

Introduction to Meditation and Mindfulness

In the sacred journey of spiritual awakening, few practices hold as profound a place as meditation and mindfulness. These ancient disciplines form the cornerstone of many spiritual traditions, acting as the gateway to deeper awareness, inner peace, and divine connection. As the first pillar of our exploration into the realms of Kundalini activation, meditation and mindfulness offer a pathway to stillness and introspection, where the soul can find its true voice and the mind can touch the infinite.

The practice of meditation is as old as human civilization itself. Historical evidence suggests that meditation was practiced in ancient cultures as a means of spiritual growth and enlightenment. The earliest records of meditation come from India, dating back to approximately 5,000 to 3,500 BCE, within the context of Hindu traditions. The Vedas, ancient Indian scriptures, contain references to Dhyana (meditation), emphasizing its importance in the pursuit of spiritual wisdom and divine connection. The practice was seen as a way to still the mind and cultivate inner silence, allowing practitioners to connect with the cosmic consciousness that underlies all existence.

One of the most revered figures in the history of meditation is Gautama

Buddha, the founder of Buddhism. Around the 6th century BCE, the young prince Siddhartha Gautama renounced his royal life in search of spiritual truth. Through intense meditation under the Bodhi tree, Siddhartha attained enlightenment and became the Buddha, the awakened one. His teachings on meditation and mindfulness, encapsulated in the practice of Vipassana (insight meditation), have inspired countless generations. Buddha's journey exemplifies the transformative power of meditation, demonstrating how deep introspection can lead to profound spiritual awakening.

In the mystical traditions of ancient China, meditation was an integral part of Taoist practices. The Tao Te Ching, attributed to the sage Laozi, highlights the importance of stillness and mindfulness as pathways to harmony with the Tao, the ultimate source of all existence. Taoist meditation focuses on aligning oneself with the natural flow of the universe, cultivating inner peace and balance. This ancient wisdom underscores the timeless relevance of meditation as a tool for personal and spiritual transformation.

As meditation spread across cultures and continents, it took on various forms, each adapted to the unique spiritual landscapes of different traditions. In Japan, Zen Buddhism refined the practice of meditation into Zazen, or seated meditation. Zen masters such as Dogen Zenji emphasized the practice of sitting in silent awareness, allowing thoughts to arise and pass without attachment. This practice, rooted in simplicity and direct experience, aims to awaken the practitioner to the present moment and the inherent interconnectedness of all life.

The Sufi mystics of Islam also embraced meditation as a means of experiencing divine love and unity. The practice of Dhikr, or remembrance of God, involves the repetitive chanting of divine names and silent contemplation. Sufi masters like Rumi and Hafiz used poetry and music to express the ecstatic states achieved through deep meditation, celebrating the soul's journey towards union with the Beloved.

In the modern era, the practice of meditation has transcended cultural and religious boundaries, becoming a universal tool for mental, emotional, and spiritual well-being. The introduction of mindfulness meditation to the West can be largely attributed to the work of Jon Kabat-Zinn, who developed

Mindfulness-Based Stress Reduction (MBSR) in the late 20th century. This secular approach to meditation emphasizes present-moment awareness and non-judgmental acceptance, making the practice accessible to people from all walks of life. Kabat-Zinn's work has demonstrated the profound benefits of mindfulness for reducing stress, enhancing mental clarity, and promoting overall health.

Meditation and mindfulness are not just practices but states of being. To meditate is to enter a space of stillness where the mind can settle, and the true nature of the self can be revealed. It is in this space that the whispers of the divine can be heard, and the subtle vibrations of Kundalini energy can be felt. Mindfulness, the art of being fully present in each moment, complements meditation by grounding us in the here and now, allowing us to experience life with greater clarity and depth.

Imagine sitting in a serene space, free from the distractions of daily life. As you close your eyes and take a deep breath, you begin to feel a sense of calm wash over you. The rhythm of your breath becomes a focal point, anchoring your awareness in the present moment. In this state of quietude, you become attuned to the subtle sensations within your body, the gentle rise and fall of your chest, the beat of your heart, and the flow of energy coursing through your veins. This is the essence of meditation—a journey inward, where the boundaries of the self dissolve, and you merge with the infinite.

Mindfulness extends this awareness into every aspect of life, transforming ordinary moments into opportunities for spiritual growth. Whether you are walking in nature, savoring a meal, or engaging in conversation, mindfulness invites you to be fully present, to experience each moment with an open heart and a clear mind. This practice cultivates a deep sense of gratitude and appreciation for the simple beauty of existence, enriching your life and enhancing your spiritual journey.

As you delve into the teachings of this chapter, you will be guided through various techniques and practices to cultivate meditation and mindfulness. You will learn to still the mind, deepen your awareness, and connect with the divine energy within. These practices will serve as the foundation for your journey of Kundalini activation, preparing you to harness the transformative power of this sacred energy.

Let the wisdom of the ages inspire you as you embark on this path of inner exploration. Embrace the stillness, listen to the whispers of your soul, and allow the light of mindfulness to illuminate your journey. In the sanctuary of meditation, may you find the peace, clarity, and divine connection that you seek, awakening to the boundless potential that resides within you.

The journey of meditation and mindfulness is one of profound discovery, a sacred path that leads inward to the very essence of our being. It is through dedicated practice and disciplined techniques that we can still the mind, awaken the soul, and connect with the divine energy that flows within us. In this chapter, we will explore various techniques and practices designed to cultivate meditation and mindfulness, each rich with detail and imbued with a mystical tone, inspiring you to delve deeper into your spiritual journey.

Breath Awareness Meditation

One of the simplest yet most powerful techniques for cultivating mindfulness and meditation is breath awareness. This practice involves focusing your attention on the natural rhythm of your breath, using it as an anchor to the present moment. Begin by finding a quiet, comfortable place to sit. Close your eyes and take a few deep breaths, allowing your body to relax. As you settle into a natural breathing rhythm, direct your attention to the sensation of the breath as it enters and leaves your nostrils.

Imagine your breath as a gentle wave, flowing in and out with ease. With each inhale, feel the cool air filling your lungs, and with each exhale, feel the warmth leaving your body. If your mind begins to wander, gently bring your focus back to your breath, using it as a tether to the present. This simple practice can deepen your awareness, calm your mind, and open the doorway to deeper states of meditation.

Mantra meditation is an ancient practice that uses the repetition of a sacred word or phrase to focus the mind and elevate spiritual awareness. Choose a mantra that resonates with you; it could be a traditional Sanskrit word like

"Om" or "So Hum," or a phrase that holds personal significance. Find a quiet place to sit, close your eyes, and begin to repeat your chosen mantra silently or aloud.

As you chant the mantra, allow its sound and vibration to fill your being, resonating with the energy centers within you. Feel the mantra reverberating through your body, mind, and spirit, dissolving any distractions or negativity. With continued practice, the mantra becomes a powerful tool for transcending the mind's chatter, drawing you into a state of deep inner peace and connection with the divine.

Guided visualization is a technique that uses the power of the mind to create vivid, immersive experiences, enhancing meditation and mindfulness. Begin by sitting or lying down in a comfortable position, closing your eyes, and taking a few deep breaths to relax. Imagine yourself in a serene, beautiful place, such as a tranquil forest, a sunlit beach, or a peaceful mountain meadow. Engage all your senses to create a detailed mental image: feel the warmth of the sun on your skin, hear the gentle rustling of leaves, and smell the fresh, fragrant air.

As you immerse yourself in this scene, allow the tranquility and beauty of your surroundings to fill your heart and mind. Visualize the divine energy flowing through you, connecting you to the natural world and the cosmos. Guided visualization can deepen your meditation practice, helping you access profound states of relaxation and spiritual insight.

Body scan meditation is a practice that enhances mindfulness by bringing awareness to different parts of the body. Begin by lying down in a comfortable position and closing your eyes. Take a few deep breaths, allowing your body to relax. Starting at the top of your head, slowly direct your attention to each part of your body, noticing any sensations, tension, or areas of relaxation.

Imagine a wave of warm, healing light flowing through each part of your body, releasing any tension and bringing a sense of peace and comfort. As you move your attention down through your body, from your head to your toes, allow this light to fill you with a sense of calm and well-being. This practice can enhance your body awareness, reduce stress, and deepen your connection to your physical and spiritual self.

Mindful walking is a practice that brings meditation into motion, combining physical movement with present-moment awareness. Find a quiet place where you can walk without distractions. Begin by standing still, taking a few deep breaths, and grounding yourself in the present moment. As you start to walk, focus your attention on the sensations of your body: the feel of your feet touching the ground, the movement of your legs, and the rhythm of your breath.

Walk slowly and deliberately, allowing each step to bring you into the here and now. Notice the sights, sounds, and smells around you, fully engaging with your environment. Mindful walking can be a powerful way to cultivate mindfulness in everyday life, bringing a sense of peace and clarity to your daily activities.

Loving-kindness meditation, also known as Metta meditation, is a practice that cultivates compassion and universal love. Begin by sitting comfortably and closing your eyes. Take a few deep breaths, allowing your heart to open. Silently repeat phrases of loving-kindness, such as "May I be happy, may I be healthy, may I be safe, may I live with ease."

After directing these phrases toward yourself, extend them to others: first to loved ones, then to neutral people, and finally to those with whom you have difficulties. As you repeat these phrases, imagine sending out waves of love and compassion, enveloping each person in a warm, healing light. Loving-kindness meditation can foster a deep sense of connection and empathy, transforming your relationships and your perception of the world.

Chakra meditation focuses on the energy centers within the body, known as chakras. Begin by sitting comfortably and closing your eyes. Take a few deep breaths, grounding yourself in the present moment. Visualize a series of energy centers along your spine, each one associated with a specific color and quality.

Starting at the base of your spine, visualize the Root Chakra as a glowing red orb of light. Imagine this light expanding and filling the area with warmth and stability. Move upward to the Sacral Chakra, visualizing an orange orb of light, representing creativity and emotion. Continue this process with each chakra: the yellow Solar Plexus Chakra (personal power), the green Heart Chakra (love and compassion), the blue Throat Chakra (communication), the indigo Third Eye Chakra (intuition), and the violet Crown Chakra (spiritual connection).

As you focus on each chakra, visualize the energy flowing freely, bringing balance and harmony to your body, mind, and spirit. Chakra meditation can help activate and align these energy centers, enhancing your overall well-being and spiritual awareness.

In essence, the techniques and practices of meditation and mindfulness are gateways to deeper self-awareness, inner peace, and spiritual awakening. By incorporating these practices into your daily life, you can cultivate a profound connection with the divine energy that flows within you, transforming your perception of yourself and the world around you. Embrace these techniques with an open heart and a willing spirit, and let the journey of meditation and mindfulness illuminate your path to higher consciousness and spiritual enlightenment.

In the vast, intricate landscape of spiritual practices, meditation stands as a beacon of tranquility and introspection, offering countless paths to inner peace and divine connection. Across cultures and epochs, various forms of meditation have emerged, each with its unique methods and philosophies, yet all converging on the common goal of deepening awareness and expanding consciousness. This chapter explores the rich diversity of meditation practices, each one a gateway to the mystical realms within.

Originating in the ancient temples of Japan, Zen meditation, or Zazen, is a practice of seated meditation that embodies simplicity and profound stillness. Practitioners sit in a specific posture, often cross-legged with a straight spine, and focus on their breath or on the stillness itself. The essence of Zazen lies in "just sitting," where one observes thoughts and sensations without attachment or judgment. Imagine yourself in a tranquil Zen garden, the gentle rustling of bamboo leaves and the serene trickling of a stream as your only companions. In this stillness, the boundaries of the self dissolve, and you become one with the moment, experiencing the profound silence that lies beyond thought.

Vipassana, which means "insight" or "clear seeing," is one of the oldest forms of meditation, rooted in the teachings of Gautama Buddha. This practice involves observing the breath and sensations in the body, cultivating a deep awareness of the impermanent nature of all phenomena. Practitioners are encouraged to maintain equanimity, observing sensations and thoughts without reacting. Imagine sitting quietly, each breath drawing you deeper into an awareness of your body's subtle sensations. This practice reveals the transient nature of thoughts and emotions, leading to profound insights into the nature of existence and a state of liberated awareness.

Metta meditation, or Loving-Kindness meditation, originates from the Buddhist tradition and focuses on cultivating an attitude of loving-kindness towards oneself and others. Practitioners repeat phrases such as "May I be happy, may I be healthy, may I be safe, may I live with ease," first directed towards themselves, then gradually extending to loved ones, neutral individuals, and even those with whom they have conflicts. Envision sending waves of loving energy from your heart, radiating outwards to encompass all beings. This practice not only fosters compassion and empathy but also transforms negative emotions, creating a heart filled with unconditional love and peace.

Transcendental Meditation, introduced by Maharishi Mahesh Yogi, involves the silent repetition of a mantra, a specific word or sound chosen for its vibrational quality. This practice is performed for 20 minutes twice a day, allowing the mind to settle into a state of restful alertness. As you repeat the mantra, imagine descending into a peaceful, serene state, where the turbulence of thoughts calms and a deep sense of inner tranquility emerges. TM is renowned for its ability to reduce stress, enhance creativity, and promote overall well-being.

Guided visualization is a form of meditation that harnesses the power of the mind to create vivid, sensory-rich experiences. Practitioners listen to a guide who leads them through a series of mental images, often involving serene landscapes, healing light, or symbolic journeys. Picture yourself walking through an ancient forest, the dappled sunlight filtering through the trees, each step bringing you closer to a sacred temple. This practice not only enhances relaxation but also taps into the subconscious mind, facilitating healing, creativity, and spiritual insight.

Chakra meditation focuses on the seven energy centers, or chakras, within the body. Each chakra is associated with specific physical, emotional, and spiritual aspects. Practitioners visualize each chakra as a spinning wheel of light, using colors, sounds, or affirmations to activate and balance these centers. Imagine a vibrant red orb at the base of your spine, representing the Root Chakra, grounding you in stability and security. As you move your attention upwards, each chakra is illuminated and balanced, culminating in a radiant violet light at the Crown Chakra, connecting you to the divine. This practice enhances energetic balance, health, and spiritual growth.

Kundalini meditation aims to awaken the dormant Kundalini energy at the base of the spine and guide it through the chakras to achieve spiritual enlightenment. This practice involves specific breathing techniques (pranayama), mantras, and physical postures (asanas) to activate and direct this energy. Visualize a coiled serpent at the base of your spine, slowly uncoiling and rising through each chakra, bringing transformative energy and heightened consciousness. The awakening of Kundalini energy leads to profound spiritual experiences and an expanded state of awareness.

Mindfulness meditation, rooted in Buddhist teachings, focuses on cultivating present-moment awareness. Practitioners observe their thoughts, emotions, and sensations without judgment, bringing attention back to the present whenever the mind wanders. Imagine sitting in quiet contemplation, each breath anchoring you in the here and now, allowing you to experience the fullness of each moment. This practice enhances mental clarity, emotional resilience, and a deep sense of inner peace.

Mantra meditation involves the repetition of a sacred word or phrase to focus the mind and invoke spiritual energy. The chosen mantra is repeated silently or aloud, aligning the practitioner with its vibrational quality. Imagine chanting "Om," the primordial sound, feeling its resonance through your body and mind, creating a bridge to the divine. This practice calms the mind, enhances concentration, and elevates spiritual consciousness.

Walking meditation, often practiced in Zen Buddhism, combines the physical act of walking with mindful awareness. Practitioners walk slowly and deliberately, focusing on the sensations of each step and the rhythm of their breath. Picture yourself walking through a tranquil garden, each step a conscious act of presence, connecting you to the earth and the flow of life. This practice brings mindfulness into motion, integrating meditation with daily activity and enhancing overall awareness.

In essence, the diverse forms of meditation offer myriad paths to inner peace, spiritual growth, and divine connection. Each practice, with its unique techniques and philosophies, opens a doorway to the mystical realms within, inviting you to explore the depths of your consciousness and the expansiveness of your spirit. As you journey through these different forms of meditation, embrace the stillness, listen to the whispers of your soul, and allow the light of awareness to guide you towards a state of profound tranquility and spiritual enlightenment.

In the fast-paced whirl of modern existence, where the demands of daily life often leave us feeling fragmented and disconnected, the practice of mindfulness stands as a beacon of tranquility and integration. Mindfulness, the art of being fully present in each moment, offers a pathway to deeper awareness and inner peace. It is not merely a meditative practice confined to silent retreats but a way of living that can transform our daily interactions, enhance our well-being, and connect us to the profound mysteries of existence. Embracing mindfulness in daily life can elevate even the most mundane tasks to moments of spiritual insight and joy.

At its core, mindfulness involves paying attention to the present moment with openness, curiosity, and without judgment. It is a practice of anchoring ourselves in the here and now, allowing us to experience life with greater clarity and depth. Imagine waking up in the morning and taking a few moments to simply breathe, feeling the gentle rise and fall of your chest, the warmth of the sunlight filtering through your window, and the soft rustle of the sheets. In this moment of mindful awareness, the day begins not with a rush of thoughts and worries but with a serene connection to the present.

One of the most accessible ways to incorporate mindfulness into daily life is through mindful breathing. Throughout the day, taking a few moments to focus on your breath can anchor you in the present and create a sense of calm. Picture yourself at work, feeling overwhelmed by a flurry of tasks and deadlines. By pausing and taking a few deep breaths, you can center your mind, release tension, and approach your responsibilities with a renewed sense of clarity and focus. This simple practice can transform moments of stress into opportunities for inner peace and composure.

Mindful eating is another powerful way to bring mindfulness into daily life. In our hurried lives, meals are often consumed quickly and mindlessly, robbing us of the sensory pleasures and nourishment that food provides. Imagine sitting down for a meal and taking the time to truly savor each bite. Notice the colors, textures, and flavors of the food, the way it feels in your mouth, and the sensations of chewing and swallowing. By eating mindfully, you not only enhance your enjoyment of food but also cultivate a deeper appreciation for the nourishment it provides and the effort that went into its preparation.

Incorporating mindfulness into daily routines can also transform seemingly mundane tasks into moments of meditation and insight. Consider the act of washing dishes. Instead of viewing it as a chore to be hurried through, approach it with mindful awareness. Feel the warmth of the water on your hands, the texture of the soap bubbles, and the smooth surface of the dishes. By fully engaging with the task at hand, you create a space for stillness and presence, turning a routine activity into a practice of mindfulness.

Mindful walking is another practice that can be seamlessly integrated into daily life. Whether you are walking to work, strolling through a park, or simply moving around your home, bringing mindfulness to your steps can ground you in the present moment. Pay attention to the sensations in your feet as they touch the ground, the rhythm of your gait, and the movement of your body. Notice the sights, sounds, and smells around you, allowing yourself to be fully immersed in the experience of walking. This practice not only enhances physical awareness but also fosters a deeper connection to your environment and a sense of unity with the world around you.

Mindfulness can also enrich our interactions with others, fostering deeper connections and empathy. Imagine engaging in a conversation with a friend or colleague and being fully present, listening with your whole being rather than planning your next response or getting distracted by your thoughts. By giving your full attention to the person you are with, you create a space of genuine connection and understanding. This practice of mindful communication can deepen relationships, resolve conflicts, and enhance mutual respect and compassion.

The practice of mindfulness extends beyond individual moments to encompass a mindful approach to life as a whole. It involves cultivating a mindful attitude, where each experience is approached with openness and curiosity. Imagine facing a challenging situation, such as a disagreement at work or a personal setback, with a mindful attitude. Instead of reacting with frustration or anger, you pause, take a deep breath, and observe your thoughts and emotions with compassion and non-judgment. This mindful approach allows you to respond with greater wisdom and equanimity, transforming challenges into opportunities for growth and learning.

Mindfulness also plays a crucial role in enhancing self-awareness and personal growth. By observing our thoughts, emotions, and behaviors with mindful attention, we gain deeper insights into our patterns and conditioning. This self-awareness empowers us to make conscious choices, break free from habitual reactions, and cultivate positive qualities such as patience, kindness, and resilience. Imagine journaling at the end of the day, reflecting on your experiences with mindfulness. You observe moments of joy and challenge, noting how you responded and what you learned. This practice of mindful reflection can illuminate your inner landscape, guiding you towards greater self-understanding and personal transformation.

In essence, the role of mindfulness in daily life is to bring us into a state of full presence and connection, transforming ordinary moments into opportunities for spiritual insight and growth. By integrating mindfulness into our daily routines, interactions, and attitudes, we cultivate a deeper sense of peace, clarity, and fulfillment. This practice invites us to embrace life with an open heart and a clear mind, allowing the beauty and mystery of each moment to unfold before us.

As you journey through the teachings of mindfulness, let this practice inspire you to live with greater awareness and intention. Embrace the present moment, listen to the whispers of your soul, and allow the light of mindfulness to guide you towards a deeper connection with yourself and the world around you. In the sacred space of mindfulness, may you find the peace, clarity, and divine connection that you seek, awakening to the boundless potential that resides within you.

In the serene stillness of the present moment lies a profound power that can transform our lives in ways both subtle and profound. This power, accessible to each of us through the practice of mindfulness, offers a pathway to enhanced well-being, deeper connection, and spiritual awakening. By weaving mindfulness into the fabric of our daily existence, we unlock a multitude of benefits that touch every aspect of our being. This chapter explores the rich tapestry of benefits that mindfulness brings, inviting you to embrace this practice with an open heart and a receptive spirit.

One of the most immediate and tangible benefits of mindfulness is its ability to reduce stress and anxiety. In the fast-paced whirl of modern life, our minds are often caught in a relentless cycle of worries, planning, and rumination. Mindfulness acts as a gentle anchor, bringing us back to the present moment and allowing us to break free from the grip of anxious thoughts. Imagine sitting quietly, focusing on your breath, and allowing the tension in your body to melt away. As your mind settles, a sense of calm and clarity emerges, replacing the turbulence with a tranquil awareness. This practice not only soothes the mind but also has a profound impact on the body, lowering stress hormones, reducing blood pressure, and promoting overall health.

Beyond its stress-relieving effects, mindfulness enhances emotional resilience and well-being. By cultivating a non-judgmental awareness of our thoughts and emotions, we learn to respond to life's challenges with greater equanimity and wisdom. Picture encountering a difficult situation, such as a disagreement with a colleague or a personal setback. Through mindfulness, you observe your emotions without being swept away by them, allowing you to respond with clarity and compassion rather than reactivity. This practice builds emotional strength, helping us navigate the ups and downs of life with a steady heart and a balanced mind.

Mindfulness also fosters a deep sense of self-awareness and personal growth. By turning our attention inward, we gain insights into our habitual patterns of thought and behavior. This heightened self-awareness empowers us to make conscious choices, break free from limiting habits, and cultivate positive qualities such as patience, kindness, and gratitude. Imagine journaling at the end of the day, reflecting on your experiences with mindful attention. You observe moments of joy and challenge, noting how you responded and what you learned. This practice illuminates your inner landscape, guiding you towards greater self-understanding and personal transformation.

Another profound benefit of mindfulness is its ability to deepen our connection with others. In a world where interactions are often rushed and superficial, mindfulness invites us to be fully present with those we encounter. Imagine engaging in a conversation with a friend, giving your full attention to their words and emotions. By listening with an open heart and a clear mind, you create a space of genuine connection and empathy. This practice of mindful communication strengthens relationships, fosters mutual understanding, and enhances the quality of our interactions.

Mindfulness also enriches our sensory experiences, allowing us to fully savor the beauty and wonder of life. When we bring mindful awareness to our surroundings, we awaken to the richness of the present moment. Picture yourself walking in nature, noticing the vibrant colors of the leaves, the intricate patterns of the bark, and the symphony of birdsong. Each step becomes a dance with the natural world, each breath a communion with the living landscape. This heightened sensory awareness not only enhances our enjoyment of life but also cultivates a deep sense of gratitude and appreciation for the simple pleasures that often go unnoticed.

On a deeper level, mindfulness opens the door to spiritual awakening and connection with the divine. By quieting the mind and turning our focus inward, we create a space for the whispers of the soul to be heard. In this stillness, we touch the infinite, experiencing a sense of unity with the cosmos. Imagine meditating in a serene space, the boundaries of the self dissolving as you merge with the boundless expanse of consciousness. This practice of mindfulness transcends the limitations of the ego, revealing the interconnectedness of all life and the sacredness of each moment.

Moreover, mindfulness has been shown to enhance cognitive function and creativity. By bringing our full attention to the task at hand, we improve our focus, memory, and problem-solving abilities. Imagine working on a creative project, your mind fully immersed in the flow of ideas and inspiration. Through mindfulness, distractions fade away, and a state of effortless concentration emerges, allowing your creativity to flourish. This practice not only enhances productivity but also brings a sense of joy and fulfillment to our endeavors.

In essence, the benefits of mindfulness are vast and varied, touching every aspect of our lives with a gentle, transformative power. By embracing mindfulness, we cultivate a deep sense of presence, clarity, and connection, enriching our relationships, enhancing our well-being, and awakening to the profound beauty of existence. As you journey through the teachings of mindfulness, let this practice inspire you to live with greater awareness and intention. Embrace the present moment, listen to the whispers of your soul, and allow the light of mindfulness to guide you towards a deeper connection with yourself, others, and the divine. In the sacred space of mindfulness, may you find the peace, clarity, and joy that you seek, awakening to the boundless potential that resides within you.

In the timeless pursuit of spiritual enlightenment, meditation and mindfulness stand as pillars of transformative practice, guiding seekers towards deeper awareness and a profound connection with the divine. These practices, though ancient, offer pathways to spiritual awakening that are as relevant today as they were thousands of years ago. Through disciplined practice, meditation and mindfulness unveil the mysteries of the soul, illuminate the path to self-realization, and foster a deep sense of unity with the cosmos. This chapter delves into the intricate ways in which these practices contribute to spiritual awakening, enriching our lives with detailed descriptions and inspiring examples.

The Inner Journey of Meditation

Meditation is often likened to an inner pilgrimage, a journey into the depths of the self where the boundaries of the physical world dissolve, revealing the vast expanse of consciousness. Through meditation, we cultivate a state of deep stillness and focused awareness, creating a space where the mind can settle and the soul can emerge. This practice serves as a gateway to spiritual awakening, allowing us to transcend the limitations of the ego and experience the infinite nature of our true being.

Imagine sitting in a quiet, sacred space, the soft glow of candlelight casting gentle shadows on the walls. As you close your eyes and focus on your breath, the distractions of the external world begin to fade away. With each inhale, you draw in the life force of the universe, and with each exhale, you release tension and negativity. In this state of deep relaxation, your mind becomes a calm, clear lake, reflecting the purity of your inner self.

In this meditative stillness, profound insights often arise. The layers of conditioned thoughts and emotions peel away, revealing the essence of who you truly are. This is the process of self-realization, where the divine spark within is uncovered, illuminating your path to spiritual enlightenment. Historical figures like Gautama Buddha experienced such profound transformations through meditation. Under the Bodhi tree, Buddha's deep meditation led to his enlightenment, where he realized the truths of existence and the nature of suffering, providing a timeless example of meditation's power to awaken the soul.

Mindfulness: The Art of Present-Moment Awareness

While meditation often involves sitting in stillness, mindfulness extends this awareness into every aspect of daily life. It is the practice of being fully present in each moment, observing our thoughts, emotions, and sensations without judgment. This state of heightened awareness is a powerful tool for spiritual awakening, as it anchors us in the present and reveals the sacredness of each moment.

Consider the act of walking mindfully through a forest. Each step is deliberate and conscious, the crunch of leaves underfoot and the scent of pine in the air fully engaging your senses. As you walk, you become aware of the interconnectedness of all life—the trees, the birds, the earth beneath your feet. This mindful awareness opens your heart to the beauty and wonder of the natural world, fostering a deep sense of gratitude and reverence.

Mindfulness also invites us to observe our inner landscape with curiosity and compassion. By paying attention to our thoughts and emotions as they arise, we gain insights into our habitual patterns and conditioning. This self-awareness is a crucial aspect of spiritual awakening, as it allows us to break free from the cycles of reactivity and align our actions with our higher self. The teachings of Thich Nhat Hanh, a renowned Vietnamese Zen master, emphasize the transformative power of mindfulness. His practice of "mindfulness in every step" encourages us to live fully in the present, seeing each moment as an opportunity for spiritual growth.

The Alchemy of Meditation and Mindfulness

When combined, meditation and mindfulness create a powerful alchemy that accelerates spiritual awakening. Meditation provides the foundation of stillness and inner peace, while mindfulness extends this state into every aspect of life, allowing us to maintain a continuous connection with our true self. Together, they cultivate a deep sense of presence, clarity, and compassion, qualities that are essential for spiritual growth.

This dynamic interplay can be seen in the practice of mindful meditation. Begin by sitting in a comfortable position and focusing on your breath, allowing your mind to settle into a state of calm. As thoughts and emotions arise, observe them with mindfulness, without getting caught up in their narrative. This practice trains the mind to remain present and equanimous, even in the face of distractions and challenges.

The benefits of this combined practice are profound. By cultivating mindfulness within meditation, we learn to navigate the complexities of our inner world with greater ease and grace. This inner stability translates into our daily lives, enabling us to approach each moment with a sense of calm and clarity. The writings of Pema Chödrön, an American Buddhist nun, beautifully illustrate this integration. Her teachings on "comfortable with uncertainty" emphasize the importance of embracing the present moment with openness and courage, a key aspect of spiritual awakening.

Transcending the Ego

One of the central goals of spiritual awakening is the transcendence of the ego—the false self that is constructed from our thoughts, beliefs, and experiences. Meditation and mindfulness play a crucial role in this process by helping us recognize and detach from the ego's illusions. Through these practices, we gain a direct experience of our true nature, which is beyond the limitations of the ego.

In meditation, as we delve deeper into stillness, we begin to observe the patterns of the ego with detachment. The constant stream of thoughts, the judgments, and the fears are seen for what they are—temporary and not truly who we are. This realization is profoundly liberating, as it frees us from the grip of the ego and opens us to the boundless nature of our true self.

Mindfulness reinforces this process by bringing the awareness cultivated in meditation into our everyday lives. By observing our reactions and behaviors with mindfulness, we can see how the ego influences our actions and relationships. This awareness allows us to make conscious choices that align with our higher self, gradually diminishing the ego's hold over us. The teachings of Eckhart Tolle, particularly in his book "The Power of Now," highlight the transformative power of living in the present moment, free from the constraints of the ego.

A Gateway to Divine Connection

Ultimately, meditation and mindfulness serve as gateways to a deeper connection with the divine. Through these practices, we awaken to the sacredness of each moment and the interconnectedness of all life. This spiritual awakening is not a destination but an ongoing journey, a continuous unfolding of our true nature.

Imagine sitting in meditation, the boundaries of your physical self dissolving as you merge with the infinite expanse of consciousness. In this state, you feel a profound sense of unity with all that is—a direct experience of the divine presence. This realization transforms your perception of the world, allowing you to see the divine in every being, every situation, and every moment.

Mindfulness further deepens this connection by bringing this awareness into daily life. Each interaction, each task, becomes an opportunity to experience the divine. Whether you are washing dishes, walking in nature, or engaging in conversation, mindfulness invites you to be fully present and open to the sacredness of each experience. This practice cultivates a deep sense of gratitude and reverence, enriching your spiritual journey.

In essence, meditation and mindfulness are powerful practices that contribute to spiritual awakening by cultivating stillness, presence, and self-awareness. These practices help us transcend the limitations of the ego, deepen our connection with the divine, and awaken to the infinite potential within us. As you embrace the teachings of meditation and mindfulness, may you be inspired to explore the depths of your inner world, awaken to your true nature, and experience the boundless beauty of spiritual awakening.

The practice of meditation and mindfulness transcends cultural and spiritual boundaries, offering profound benefits that resonate with both scientific inquiry and spiritual wisdom. These ancient practices, grounded in millennia of tradition, have gained widespread recognition in modern science for their transformative effects on the mind, body, and spirit. This chapter delves into the scientific and spiritual benefits of meditation and mindfulness, weaving detailed descriptions and inspiring examples to illuminate their profound impact on our lives.

Scientific Benefits of Meditation and Mindfulness

Modern scientific research has extensively documented the myriad benefits of meditation and mindfulness, validating what spiritual traditions have long known. One of the most well-documented benefits is the reduction of stress. Chronic stress, a pervasive issue in contemporary society, has been linked to numerous health problems, including cardiovascular disease, diabetes, and mental health disorders. Meditation and mindfulness practices have been shown to reduce the production of stress hormones such as cortisol and adrenaline, promoting a state of relaxation and calm.

Imagine, for instance, a busy professional who regularly practices mindfulness. By taking just a few minutes each day to focus on their breath and observe their thoughts without judgment, they experience a significant reduction in stress. This practice not only improves their mental health but also lowers their risk of stress-related illnesses, enhancing their overall well-being.

Another key benefit is the improvement in cognitive function. Studies have shown that regular meditation can enhance attention, memory, and executive function. One landmark study conducted by researchers at Harvard Medical School found that mindfulness meditation increases the density of gray matter in the hippocampus, an area of the brain associated with learning and memory, and reduces gray matter density in the amygdala, which is associated with stress and anxiety. These changes in brain structure underscore the profound impact of meditation on cognitive health.

Consider a student who incorporates meditation into their daily routine. They find that their ability to concentrate during classes improves, their memory retention is enhanced, and they can approach exams with a calm and focused mind. This cognitive enhancement not only boosts their academic performance but also fosters a more balanced and stress-free approach to learning.

The benefits of meditation extend to emotional well-being as well. Mindfulness practices have been shown to increase emotional resilience, reduce symptoms of depression and anxiety, and enhance overall mood. A study published in the journal "JAMA Internal Medicine" found that mindfulness meditation programs can lead to significant reductions in symptoms of depression and anxiety, comparable to the effects of antidepressant medications.

Imagine someone struggling with anxiety who begins a regular mindfulness practice. Over time, they notice a decrease in their anxiety symptoms, an increased ability to manage stressful situations, and a greater sense of emotional stability. This transformation not only improves their mental health but also enriches their relationships and overall quality of life.

Additionally, meditation has been linked to improved physical health. It can lower blood pressure, enhance immune function, and promote better sleep. A study published in the journal "Circulation" found that individuals who practiced transcendental meditation had a significant reduction in blood pressure, comparable to the effects of antihypertensive medications. This evidence highlights the holistic benefits of meditation, bridging the gap between mind and body health.

Spiritual Benefits of Meditation and Mindfulness

While the scientific benefits of meditation and mindfulness are profound, the spiritual benefits are equally transformative, offering a pathway to deeper self-awareness, inner peace, and a profound connection with the divine.

Meditation and mindfulness cultivate a state of inner stillness, where the mind's chatter quiets, and the soul's whispers can be heard. This inner stillness is a fertile ground for spiritual insights and revelations, allowing us to connect with our true nature and the greater mysteries of existence. Imagine sitting in meditation, the mind settling into a serene silence, and feeling a deep sense of peace and unity with the universe. This experience of inner stillness is a gateway to spiritual awakening, revealing the boundless nature of our true self.

These practices also foster a deep sense of presence and connection with the present moment. By fully immersing ourselves in the here and now, we transcend the limitations of the past and future, experiencing the sacredness of each moment. This mindful presence opens our hearts to the beauty and wonder of life, cultivating a sense of gratitude and reverence for the present. Imagine walking mindfully through a forest, each step a conscious act of presence, and feeling a profound connection to the natural world and the divine energy that flows through it. This practice of mindfulness transforms ordinary moments into sacred experiences, enriching our spiritual journey.

Meditation and mindfulness also enhance our capacity for compassion and empathy. By observing our thoughts and emotions with non-judgmental awareness, we cultivate a deeper understanding of ourselves and others. This self-awareness fosters a sense of compassion and empathy, allowing us to connect with others on a deeper level. Imagine engaging in a loving-kindness meditation, sending thoughts of love and compassion to yourself and others, and feeling a profound sense of connection and unity. This practice not only enriches our relationships but also aligns us with the universal principles of love and compassion.

Furthermore, these practices facilitate the transcendence of the ego and the realization of our true nature. By observing the patterns of the ego with mindful awareness, we recognize that our true self is beyond the limitations of thoughts, beliefs, and identities. This realization is profoundly liberating, allowing us to experience the infinite nature of our being. Imagine sitting in meditation, observing the flow of thoughts and emotions, and experiencing a profound sense of detachment and freedom. This transcendence of the ego reveals the interconnectedness of all life, fostering a sense of unity and oneness with the cosmos.

In essence, the benefits of meditation and mindfulness are vast and varied, touching every aspect of our being with a gentle, transformative power. These practices enhance our mental, emotional, and physical health, fostering a state of holistic well-being. They also open the door to spiritual awakening, revealing the profound mysteries of our true nature and the divine connection that unites all existence.

As you embrace the teachings of meditation and mindfulness, may you be inspired to explore the depths of your inner world, awaken to your true nature, and experience the boundless beauty of spiritual awakening. In the sacred space of mindfulness, may you find the peace, clarity, and divine connection that you seek, awakening to the boundless potential that resides within you.

Pillar Two

Introduction to Breathwork and Pranayama

In the sacred tapestry of spiritual practices, breathwork holds a place of profound significance. It is the bridge between the body and the spirit, the thread that connects the physical with the divine. Through the conscious control of our breath, we can unlock the door to deeper awareness, inner tranquility, and spiritual awakening. This chapter introduces the mystical art of breathwork and Pranayama, offering detailed descriptions and inspiring examples to illuminate their transformative power.

Breath is life. From the moment we take our first breath at birth to our final exhalation, the breath is a constant companion, sustaining us and connecting us to the universal life force. In many spiritual traditions, the breath is seen as a sacred tool for spiritual growth and transformation. In Sanskrit, the word "Prana" means life force or vital energy, and "Ayama" means extension or control. Pranayama, therefore, is the practice of extending and controlling the life force through breath.

Imagine sitting in a quiet, sacred space, the air around you charged with a sense of tranquility and stillness. As you close your eyes and begin to focus on your breath, you become aware of its gentle rhythm, the rise and fall of your chest, and the cool air entering your nostrils. With each inhale, you draw in the life force of the universe, and with each exhale, you release tension and negativity. This conscious awareness of breath is the foundation of Pranayama, a practice that can transform your physical, mental, and spiritual well-being.

The Science of Breath

Modern science has begun to uncover the profound effects of breathwork on the body and mind. Research has shown that controlled breathing can reduce stress, lower blood pressure, enhance cognitive function, and improve overall health. When we engage in deep, rhythmic breathing, we activate the parasympathetic nervous system, which promotes relaxation and counteracts the stress response. This physiological shift not only calms the mind but also supports the body's natural healing processes.

Consider a person struggling with anxiety who begins practicing deep diaphragmatic breathing. Over time, they notice a significant reduction in their anxiety symptoms, an increased ability to manage stress, and a greater sense of emotional stability. This transformation highlights the power of breathwork to influence our mental and emotional states, fostering a sense of inner peace and resilience.

Pranayama encompasses a variety of techniques, each with its unique benefits and purposes. These techniques range from simple breath awareness to more advanced practices that involve breath retention and specific breathing patterns. Here, we explore some foundational Pranayama practices that can be incorporated into daily life.

Nadi Shodhana, or alternate nostril breathing, is a powerful technique for balancing the body's energy channels (nadis) and calming the mind. To practice Nadi Shodhana, sit in a comfortable position with your spine straight. Close your right nostril with your right thumb and inhale deeply through your left nostril. Then close your left nostril with your right ring finger and exhale through your right nostril. Inhale through your right nostril, close it with your thumb, and exhale through your left nostril. This completes one cycle.

Imagine the breath flowing effortlessly through your nostrils, cleansing and balancing your energy channels. With each inhale, you draw in fresh prana, and with each exhale, you release stagnant energy. This practice not only calms the mind but also enhances mental clarity and emotional balance.

Kapalabhati, or skull shining breath, is a vigorous breathing technique that purifies the mind and body. It involves forceful exhalations followed by passive inhalations. To practice Kapalabhati, sit comfortably with your spine straight. Take a deep inhale and then forcefully exhale through your nose, pulling your navel towards your spine. Allow the inhalation to occur passively, and then repeat the forceful exhalation.

Envision each exhale as a powerful cleansing wave, expelling toxins and impurities from your body and mind. This practice energizes the body, clears the mind, and enhances overall vitality. It is particularly beneficial for increasing lung capacity and boosting mental focus.

Ujjayi, or victorious breath, is a calming and soothing breath technique often used in yoga practice. It involves breathing through the nose while slightly constricting the throat, creating a soft, whispering sound. To practice Ujjayi, sit comfortably and take a deep inhale through your nose, slightly constricting the back of your throat. Exhale through your nose with the same constriction, maintaining a steady, rhythmic breath.

Imagine the breath flowing smoothly and steadily, like the gentle waves of the ocean. The sound of Ujjayi breath creates a sense of inner calm and focus, allowing you to connect deeply with your inner self. This practice enhances concentration, reduces stress, and promotes a sense of inner peace.

Bhramari, or bee breath, is a soothing technique that calms the mind and reduces anxiety. It involves making a humming sound during exhalation, resembling the buzzing of a bee. To practice Bhramari, sit comfortably with your spine straight. Close your eyes and take a deep inhale through your nose. As you exhale, gently press your index fingers on your ears and make a humming sound.

Envision the soothing vibrations of the humming sound resonating throughout your body, calming your mind and releasing tension. This practice induces a state of deep relaxation, reduces stress, and enhances emotional stability.

Breathwork and Pranayama can be seamlessly integrated into daily life, offering moments of calm and clarity amidst the busyness of everyday activities. Consider starting your day with a few minutes of Nadi Shodhana to balance your energy and set a calm, focused tone for the day. Throughout the day, practice deep diaphragmatic breathing whenever you feel stressed or overwhelmed, allowing your breath to ground you in the present moment.

Incorporating breathwork into your yoga practice can also enhance its benefits. Use Ujjayi breath during your yoga asanas to maintain focus and deepen your connection to each movement. End your practice with a few rounds of Bhramari to induce a state of deep relaxation and inner peace.

The Spiritual Dimension of Breathwork

Beyond its physical and mental benefits, breathwork holds a profound spiritual significance. In many spiritual traditions, the breath is seen as a sacred tool for connecting with the divine and awakening the inner self. Pranayama practices are often used to prepare the mind and body for deeper states of meditation and spiritual awareness.

Imagine sitting in meditation, your breath flowing effortlessly and rhythmically. As you focus on your breath, you feel a sense of unity with the universal life force, a profound connection to the divine essence that flows through all of creation. This experience of oneness transcends the boundaries of the physical world, revealing the infinite nature of your true self.

In essence, breathwork and Pranayama are powerful practices that bridge the gap between the physical and the spiritual, offering profound benefits for the body, mind, and soul. By cultivating a conscious awareness of our breath, we can transform our physical health, enhance our mental clarity, and deepen our spiritual connection. As you embrace the teachings of breathwork, may you be inspired to explore the depths of your inner world, awaken to your true nature, and experience the boundless beauty of spiritual awakening.

Breath is the bridge between the body and the spirit, the lifeline that connects our physical existence to the divine essence within us. Pranayama, the ancient art of breath control, offers profound techniques for enhancing our physical health, mental clarity, and spiritual growth. This chapter provides a step-by-step guide to basic Pranayama exercises, inviting you to explore the mystical power of breath and inspiring you to integrate these practices into your daily life.

Nadi Shodhana (Alternate Nostril Breathing)

Nadi Shodhana, or alternate nostril breathing, is a foundational Pranayama practice that balances the body's energy channels (nadis) and calms the mind. This exercise is particularly beneficial for reducing stress and enhancing mental clarity.

Step-by-Step Guide:

1. Preparation:
   - Find a quiet, comfortable place to sit. Sit cross-legged on the floor or on a chair with your feet flat on the ground. Keep your spine straight and your shoulders relaxed. Close your eyes and take a few deep breaths to center yourself.

2. Hand Position:
   - Lift your right hand and place your thumb gently on your right nostril. Your index and middle fingers can rest on your forehead, while your ring finger and little finger are positioned near your left nostril.

3. Initial Inhale:
   - Close your right nostril with your thumb and inhale deeply through your left nostril. Feel the cool air filling your lungs, energizing your body.

4. Switching Sides:

- Close your left nostril with your ring finger, release your right nostril, and exhale slowly through your right nostril. Feel the warmth of the air as it leaves your body, carrying away tension.

5. Continue the Cycle:

- Inhale deeply through your right nostril, then close your right nostril and exhale through your left nostril. This completes one cycle.

- Repeat this process for 5-10 minutes, focusing on the rhythmic flow of your breath and the balance it brings to your body and mind.

Imagine practicing Nadi Shodhana in a serene garden, the gentle sounds of nature around you. As you breathe through each nostril, you feel a sense of harmony and balance, the breath flowing like a gentle river, cleansing and rejuvenating your energy.

Kapalabhati (Skull Shining Breath)

Kapalabhati, or skull shining breath, is a vigorous Pranayama technique that purifies the mind and body. It involves forceful exhalations followed by passive inhalations, stimulating the respiratory system and energizing the body.

Step-by-Step Guide:

1. Preparation:

- Sit comfortably with your spine straight and shoulders relaxed. Place your hands on your knees with palms facing upward. Close your eyes and take a few deep breaths to settle your mind.

2. Initial Inhale:

- Take a deep inhale through both nostrils, filling your lungs completely.

3. Forceful Exhalations:

- Exhale forcefully through your nose, contracting your abdominal muscles to push the air out. Allow the inhalation to occur passively, without any effort.

- Focus on the forceful exhalations, creating a rhythm. Begin with 20 exhalations, gradually increasing to 50-100 as you become more comfortable with the practice.

4. Completion:

- After completing your cycles of exhalations, take a deep inhale, hold the breath for a few seconds, and then exhale slowly. Sit quietly for a few moments, observing the sensations in your body.

Imagine practicing Kapalabhati at dawn, the rising sun casting a golden glow around you. Each forceful exhalation feels like a burst of light, clearing away the darkness and filling you with vibrant energy. As you complete the practice, you feel invigorated and ready to embrace the day with clarity and enthusiasm.

Ujjayi (Victorious Breath)

Ujjayi, or victorious breath, is a soothing and rhythmic Pranayama technique often used in yoga practice. It involves breathing through the nose while slightly constricting the throat, creating a soft, whispering sound.

Step-by-Step Guide:

1. Preparation:

- Sit comfortably with your spine straight and shoulders relaxed. Close your eyes and take a few deep breaths to center yourself.

2. Throat Constriction:

- Inhale deeply through your nose, slightly constricting the back of your throat as if you were whispering. This creates a soft, ocean-like sound.

3. Exhale with Sound:

- Exhale through your nose with the same constriction, maintaining the gentle, whispering sound. Focus on creating a steady, rhythmic breath.

4. Continue the Rhythm:

- Continue breathing in this manner for 5-10 minutes, focusing on the sound and the sensation of the breath moving through your throat.

Imagine practicing Ujjayi in a quiet room, candlelight casting flickering shadows on the walls. The soft, ocean-like sound of your breath creates a sense of inner calm and focus. As you continue, you feel a deep connection to your inner self, the breath guiding you to a place of serenity and peace.

Bhramari (Bee Breath)

Bhramari, or bee breath, is a calming Pranayama technique that reduces anxiety and induces a state of deep relaxation. It involves making a humming sound during exhalation, resembling the buzzing of a bee.

Step-by-Step Guide:

1. Preparation:

- Sit comfortably with your spine straight and shoulders relaxed. Close your eyes and take a few deep breaths to settle your mind.

2. Inhale Deeply:

- Take a deep inhale through your nose, filling your lungs completely.

3. Exhale with Humming:

- As you exhale, press your index fingers gently on your ears and make a humming sound, similar to the buzzing of a bee. Feel the vibrations in your head and chest.

4. Continue the Practice:

- Continue this process for 5-10 minutes, focusing on the soothing vibrations and the calming effect on your mind.

Imagine practicing Bhramari in a tranquil forest, the natural sounds blending with the gentle hum of your breath. The vibrations resonate through your body, creating a sense of peace and harmony. As you continue, you feel a deep sense of relaxation and connection to the natural world.

Integrating Pranayama into Daily Life

Pranayama can be seamlessly integrated into your daily routine, providing moments of calm and clarity amidst the busyness of life. Consider starting your day with a few minutes of Nadi Shodhana to balance your energy and set a peaceful tone for the day. Use Kapalabhati to invigorate yourself during the mid-afternoon slump, and practice Ujjayi or Bhramari in the evening to unwind and prepare for restful sleep.

These practices not only enhance your physical health but also deepen your spiritual connection, guiding you towards a state of inner peace and enlightenment. As you embrace the teachings of Pranayama, may you be inspired to explore the depths of your inner world, awaken to your true nature, and experience the boundless beauty of spiritual awakening. In the sacred space of breath, may you find the peace, clarity, and divine connection that you seek, awakening to the boundless potential that resides within you.

In the sacred dance of daily life, breathwork serves as a bridge between the mundane and the mystical, grounding us in the present moment while connecting us to the divine essence within. By integrating breathwork into our daily routines, we can enhance our physical health, calm our minds, and deepen our spiritual awareness. This chapter provides detailed descriptions and inspiring examples of how to seamlessly incorporate breathwork into your everyday activities, inviting you to explore the transformative power of conscious breathing.

Morning Ritual: Awakening with Pranayama

Begin your day with a morning breathwork ritual that sets a tone of calm and clarity. As you awaken, before reaching for your phone or diving into the day's tasks, take a few moments to center yourself with a simple Pranayama practice.

Nadi Shodhana (Alternate Nostril Breathing)

1. Preparation:
   - Sit comfortably on your bed or a cushion with your spine straight. Close your eyes and take a few deep breaths to settle your mind.

2. Hand Position:
   - Place your right thumb on your right nostril, your index and middle fingers on your forehead, and your ring finger near your left nostril.

3. Initial Inhale:
   - Close your right nostril with your thumb and inhale deeply through your left nostril.

4. Switching Sides:

- Close your left nostril with your ring finger, release your right nostril, and exhale slowly through your right nostril.

5. Continue the Cycle:
- Inhale through your right nostril, close it with your thumb, and exhale through your left nostril. Repeat this process for 5-10 minutes.

Imagine the gentle morning light filtering through your window as you breathe deeply, balancing your energy and centering your mind. This practice awakens your senses and prepares you for the day ahead with a sense of peace and clarity.

Midday Recharge: Invigorating Breathwork

In the midst of a busy day, taking a few moments for breathwork can provide a much-needed boost of energy and focus. Whether you're at work, at home, or on the go, a quick breathwork session can recharge your mind and body.

Kapalabhati (Skull Shining Breath)

1. Preparation:
- Sit comfortably with your spine straight and shoulders relaxed. Place your hands on your knees with palms facing upward. Close your eyes and take a few deep breaths to settle your mind.

2. Initial Inhale:
- Take a deep inhale through both nostrils, filling your lungs completely.

3. Forceful Exhalations:
- Exhale forcefully through your nose, contracting your abdominal muscles to push the air out. Allow the inhalation to occur passively.

- Begin with 20 exhalations, gradually increasing to 50-100 as you become more comfortable.

4. Completion:

- After completing your cycles of exhalations, take a deep inhale, hold the breath for a few seconds, and then exhale slowly. Sit quietly for a few moments, observing the sensations in your body.

Imagine taking a break from your computer screen, closing your eyes, and engaging in Kapalabhati. Each forceful exhalation clears your mind and revitalizes your energy, leaving you feeling invigorated and ready to tackle the rest of your tasks with renewed focus.

Evening Wind Down: Preparing for Restful Sleep

As the day winds down, integrating breathwork into your evening routine can help you release the day's stress and prepare for restful sleep. A calming breathwork practice can signal to your body that it's time to relax and unwind.

Example Practice: Ujjayi (Victorious Breath)

1. Preparation:

- Sit or lie down in a comfortable position. Close your eyes and take a few deep breaths to settle your mind.

2. Throat Constriction:

- Inhale deeply through your nose, slightly constricting the back of your throat to create a soft, ocean-like sound.

3. Exhale with Sound:

- Exhale through your nose with the same constriction, maintaining a steady, rhythmic breath.

4. **Continue the Rhythm:**

- Continue breathing in this manner for 5-10 minutes, focusing on the soothing sound and the sensation of the breath moving through your throat.

Imagine lying in bed, the soft sound of Ujjayi breath creating a cocoon of tranquility around you. As you breathe deeply, the day's worries melt away, and you drift into a state of deep relaxation, preparing your mind and body for a night of restful sleep.

Integrating Breathwork into Daily Activities

Breathwork doesn't have to be confined to specific times of day; it can be woven into your daily activities to enhance mindfulness and presence. Here are some examples of how to incorporate breathwork into various aspects of your routine:

As you walk, whether it's during your commute or a stroll in the park, focus on your breath. Match your steps to your breath, inhaling for a set number of steps and exhaling for the same number. This practice brings mindfulness to your movement and deepens your connection to the present moment.

Imagine walking through a park, the rhythmic pattern of your breath syncing with your steps. Each inhale brings in the fresh scent of nature, and each exhale releases tension, grounding you in the beauty of your surroundings.

Set reminders on your phone to take breath breaks throughout the day. During these breaks, practice a simple breathwork technique, such as deep diaphragmatic breathing. This helps you stay centered and reduces stress.

Imagine receiving a gentle reminder on your phone, prompting you to pause and take a few deep breaths. As you do, you feel a wave of calm wash over you, resetting your mind and body for the tasks ahead.

Before each meal, take a moment to practice a few rounds of deep, conscious breathing. This not only prepares your digestive system but also enhances your awareness and appreciation of the food.

Imagine sitting down to a meal, taking a few deep breaths, and feeling gratitude for the nourishment before you. This mindful pause enriches your dining experience, allowing you to savor each bite fully.

Breathwork can be seamlessly integrated into meditation and yoga practices, enhancing their benefits and deepening your connection to the present moment.

Begin your meditation session with a few minutes of Pranayama, such as Nadi Shodhana or Ujjayi breath. This prepares your mind and body for deeper meditation, creating a state of calm and focus.

Imagine starting your meditation with alternate nostril breathing, feeling your energy balance and your mind settle. As you transition into meditation, you find it easier to maintain a state of deep stillness and awareness.

Use Ujjayi breath during your yoga practice to maintain focus and deepen your connection to each movement. Coordinate your breath with your asanas, inhaling during upward movements and exhaling during downward movements.

Imagine flowing through a series of yoga poses, the sound of your Ujjayi breath guiding your movements. Each inhale and exhale becomes a dance of breath and body, enhancing your practice and deepening your sense of inner peace.

Beyond its physical and mental benefits, breathwork holds profound spiritual significance. It is a tool for deepening your connection to the divine and awakening your inner self.

Use Bhramari breath to induce a state of deep relaxation and connect with your inner self. The soothing vibrations of the humming sound resonate through your body, creating a sense of unity with the universe.

Imagine sitting in meditation, the gentle hum of Bhramari breath creating waves of vibration through your being. As you continue, you feel a deep sense of peace and connection to the divine essence within you.

In essence, integrating breathwork into your daily routine offers a pathway to enhanced well-being, deeper mindfulness, and spiritual growth. By incorporating these practices into various aspects of your day, you can create moments of calm and clarity amidst the busyness of life. As you embrace the teachings of breathwork, may you be inspired to explore the depths of your inner world, awaken to your true nature, and experience the boundless beauty of spiritual awakening. In the sacred space of breath, may you find the peace, clarity, and divine connection that you seek, awakening to the boundless potential that resides within you.

/ Pillar Three

Physical Asanas and Movement

In the sacred dance of life, our bodies are the vessels through which we experience the world and express our innermost essence. Physical asanas and movement, integral components of yoga, offer a pathway to harmonize body, mind, and spirit, grounding us in the present while elevating our consciousness. This chapter explores the mystical power of asanas and movement, providing detailed descriptions and inspiring examples to guide you on your journey of spiritual awakening through physical practice.

Asanas, the physical postures of yoga, are more than mere exercises; they are sacred forms that channel divine energy, align the chakras, and prepare the body for deeper spiritual practices. Each asana carries its unique symbolism and energy, offering a gateway to inner transformation and self-discovery. When performed mindfully, asanas become a moving meditation, allowing the practitioner to transcend the physical realm and connect with the divine.

Tadasana (Mountain Pose)

Tadasana, or Mountain Pose, is a foundational asana that embodies the essence of stability and strength. Standing tall with feet together and arms at your sides, you become a mountain, grounded yet reaching for the sky.

Step-by-Step Guide:

1. Stand Tall:
   - Stand with your feet together or hip-width apart, grounding evenly through all four corners of your feet. Engage your thighs, lift your kneecaps, and lengthen your spine.

2. Lift and Open:
   - Inhale deeply, lifting your chest and broadening your collarbones. Let your arms hang naturally by your sides with palms facing forward.

3. Align and Center:
   - Align your head over your heart and your heart over your pelvis. Soften your gaze and breathe deeply, feeling the earth beneath you and the sky above.

Imagine standing in a serene meadow at dawn, the first rays of sunlight kissing your face. As you stand in Tadasana, you feel a deep connection to the earth, a sense of rootedness and stability. The energy of the earth flows upward through your body, meeting the expansive energy of the sky, creating a harmonious balance within you.

Flowing with Movement: Sun Salutations

Sun Salutations, or Surya Namaskar, are a dynamic sequence of asanas performed in a flowing manner. This practice honors the sun, the source of all life, and symbolizes the cyclical nature of existence. Sun Salutations are both a physical workout and a moving prayer, aligning the body with the rhythms of the universe.

Step-by-Step Guide:

1. Begin in Tadasana:

- Stand at the top of your mat in Mountain Pose, grounding yourself and setting your intention for the practice.

2. Reach Up:

- Inhale and sweep your arms overhead, joining your palms in Anjali Mudra (prayer position). Look up towards your hands, feeling a sense of openness and expansion.

3. Forward Fold:

- Exhale and hinge at your hips, folding forward with a straight spine. Let your hands come to the floor or your shins, releasing any tension in your neck.

4. Half Lift:

- Inhale and lift your torso halfway, extending your spine and looking forward. Place your hands on your shins or fingertips on the floor.

5. Plank Pose:

- Exhale and step back into Plank Pose, creating a straight line from your head to your heels. Engage your core and hold for a few breaths.

6. Chaturanga Dandasana:

- Lower your body down to the floor with control, keeping your elbows close to your sides.

7. Upward-Facing Dog:

- Inhale and lift your chest into Upward-Facing Dog, straightening your arms and opening your heart. Press the tops of your feet into the mat.

8. Downward-Facing Dog:

- Exhale and lift your hips up and back into Downward-Facing Dog. Press your hands firmly into the mat and lengthen your spine.

9. Forward Fold:

- Inhale and step forward to the top of your mat, lifting halfway with a flat back. Exhale and fold forward deeply.

10. Rise Up:

- Inhale and sweep your arms overhead, returning to standing with palms joined above your head. Exhale and lower your arms to your sides, returning to Tadasana.

Imagine performing Sun Salutations on a quiet beach at sunrise, the rhythmic sound of waves accompanying your breath. As you move through the sequence, each posture flows into the next like a graceful dance, your body aligning with the cycles of nature. With each breath, you honor the sun, feeling its warmth and vitality infusing your being.

Heart-Opening Asanas: Ustrasana (Camel Pose)

Heart-opening asanas, such as Ustrasana (Camel Pose), invite us to release emotional blockages and cultivate a sense of openness and vulnerability. These postures expand the chest, stimulate the heart chakra, and foster a deep sense of compassion and love.

Step-by-Step Guide:

1. Kneel on Your Mat:

- Begin by kneeling on your mat with your knees hip-width apart. Place your hands on your lower back for support.

2. Lift and Open:

- Inhale and lift your chest, gently arching your back. Reach your hands back to grasp your heels, pressing your hips forward.

3. Deepen the Stretch:

- Allow your head to drop back gently, opening your throat and heart. Breathe deeply, feeling the expansion in your chest.

4. Release Gently:

- After a few breaths, release your hands from your heels and slowly return to a kneeling position. Rest in Child's Pose for a few moments to integrate the experience.

Imagine practicing Ustrasana in a quiet forest clearing, the fragrance of pine trees filling the air. As you open your heart in the pose, you feel a deep sense of release and vulnerability. The energy of the earth rises to meet you, supporting and nurturing you as you expand your heart space, allowing love and compassion to flow freely.

Grounding Asanas: Virabhadrasana I (Warrior I)

Grounding asanas, such as Virabhadrasana I (Warrior I), cultivate strength, stability, and courage. These postures connect us to the earth, empowering us to face life's challenges with confidence and resilience.

Step-by-Step Guide:

1. Step Back:

- From Tadasana, step your left foot back, turning it out slightly. Bend your right knee, aligning it over your right ankle.

2. Lift and Reach:

- Inhale and lift your arms overhead, joining your palms in Anjali Mudra. Gaze forward or up towards your hands.

3. Ground and Center:

- Press firmly into both feet, grounding yourself and feeling the strength in your legs. Breathe deeply, embodying the warrior's spirit.

4. Switch Sides:

- After a few breaths, release and step forward, returning to Tadasana. Repeat on the opposite side.

Imagine practicing Warrior I on a mountaintop, the vast expanse of the landscape before you. As you ground into the pose, you feel a surge of strength and determination. The energy of the mountain flows through you, instilling a sense of resilience and empowerment.

Integrating Asanas and Movement into Daily Life

Physical asanas and mindful movement can be seamlessly integrated into your daily routine, transforming everyday activities into opportunities for spiritual practice.

Begin your day with a gentle sequence of stretches to awaken your body and mind. Incorporate movements such as Cat-Cow, Downward-Facing Dog, and Standing Forward Fold to release tension and energize your body.

Imagine starting your day with a series of gentle stretches, the morning light streaming through your window. Each movement is a mindful exploration, awakening your body and setting a tone of presence and intention for the day ahead.

Desk Yoga

Take short breaks throughout your workday to practice simple asanas at your desk. Incorporate movements such as Seated Forward Bend, Seated Spinal Twist, and Shoulder Rolls to relieve tension and maintain focus.

Imagine pausing during a busy workday to practice a seated spinal twist, feeling the tension melt away from your back and shoulders. These brief moments of movement bring a sense of clarity and calm, enhancing your productivity and well-being.

Evening Wind Down

End your day with a calming sequence of asanas to release the day's stress and prepare for restful sleep. Incorporate movements such as Child's Pose, Supine Spinal Twist, and Legs-Up-the-Wall Pose to relax your body and quiet your mind.

Imagine unwinding at the end of the day with a series of gentle, restorative poses. The soft glow of candlelight creates a serene ambiance as you stretch and breathe deeply, releasing the day's tension and inviting a sense of peace and relaxation.

Beyond their physical benefits, asanas hold profound spiritual significance. Each posture is a sacred form that channels divine energy, aligns the chakras, and prepares the body for deeper states of meditation and spiritual awareness.

Enhance your asana practice by integrating Pranayama techniques. Use Ujjayi breath during your yoga practice to maintain focus and deepen your connection to each movement. Coordinate your breath with your asanas, inhaling during upward movements and exhaling during downward movements.

Beyond their physical benefits, asanas hold profound spiritual significance.

Each posture is a sacred form that channels divine energy, aligns the chakras, and prepares the body for deeper states of meditation and spiritual awareness.

Enhance your asana practice by integrating Pranayama techniques. Use Ujjayi breath during your yoga practice to maintain focus and deepen your connection to each movement. Coordinate your breath with your asanas, inhaling during upward movements and exhaling during downward movements.

Imagine flowing through a series of yoga poses in a serene studio, the sound of your Ujjayi breath creating a rhythmic symphony that guides your movements. Each inhale lifts you into a new posture, while each exhale grounds you deeper into the present moment. This harmonious dance of breath and movement becomes a moving meditation, connecting you to the divine energy within.

Focusing on the heart chakra, or Anahata, can open pathways to love, compassion, and emotional healing. Asanas that expand the chest and open the heart are particularly beneficial for balancing this chakra.

Bhujangasana (Cobra Pose)

Bhujangasana, or Cobra Pose, is a gentle backbend that stimulates the heart chakra and promotes emotional openness.

Step-by-Step Guide:

1. Begin Prone:

- Lie face down on your mat with your legs extended and the tops of your feet pressing into the mat. Place your hands under your shoulders, elbows close to your body.

2. Lift and Open:

- Inhale and lift your chest off the ground, using the strength of your back muscles rather than pushing with your hands. Keep your elbows slightly bent and your shoulders away from your ears.

3. Expand and Breathe:

- Open your heart and gaze slightly upward, breathing deeply and feeling the expansion in your chest. Hold the pose for a few breaths before gently lowering back down.

Imagine practicing Cobra Pose in a peaceful garden, the scent of blooming flowers filling the air. As you lift into the pose, your heart opens to the sky, and you feel a wave of compassion and love wash over you. Each breath deepens this connection, fostering a sense of emotional healing and balance.

Grounding Practice: Muladhara Chakra Asanas

Grounding asanas connect us to the earth and cultivate stability, strength, and a sense of security. These poses are particularly effective for balancing the root chakra, or Muladhara.

Virabhadrasana II (Warrior II Pose)

Virabhadrasana II, or Warrior II Pose, embodies the strength and stability of a warrior, grounding us in the present moment.

Step-by-Step Guide:

1. Step Wide:

- From Tadasana, step your feet wide apart. Turn your right foot out 90 degrees and your left foot slightly in. Align your heels.

2. Bend and Ground:

- Bend your right knee over your right ankle, keeping your left leg straight and strong. Extend your arms parallel to the ground, palms facing down.

3. Focus Forward:

- Gaze over your right hand, breathing deeply and feeling the strength in your legs and core. Hold the pose for several breaths before switching sides.

Imagine practicing Warrior II on a mountaintop, the vast landscape stretching out before you. As you ground into the pose, you feel the strength and stability of the earth beneath you. Each breath anchors you in the present moment, filling you with a sense of courage and resilience.

Physical asanas and mindful movement can be seamlessly integrated into your daily routine, transforming everyday activities into opportunities for spiritual practice.

Begin your day with a gentle sequence of stretches to awaken your body and mind. Incorporate movements such as Cat-Cow, Downward-Facing Dog, and Standing Forward Fold to release tension and energize your body.

Imagine starting your day with a series of gentle stretches, the morning light streaming through your window. Each movement is a mindful exploration, awakening your body and setting a tone of presence and intention for the day ahead.

Desk Yoga

Take short breaks throughout your workday to practice simple asanas at your desk. Incorporate movements such as Seated Forward Bend, Seated Spinal Twist, and Shoulder Rolls to relieve tension and maintain focus.

Imagine pausing during a busy workday to practice a seated spinal twist, feeling the tension melt away from your back and shoulders. These brief moments of movement bring a sense of clarity and calm, enhancing your productivity and well-being.

End your day with a calming sequence of asanas to release the day's stress and prepare for restful sleep. Incorporate movements such as Child's Pose, Supine Spinal Twist, and Legs-Up-the-Wall Pose to relax your body and quiet your mind.

Imagine unwinding at the end of the day with a series of gentle, restorative poses. The soft glow of candlelight creates a serene ambiance as you stretch and breathe deeply, releasing the day's tension and inviting a sense of peace and relaxation.

The Spiritual Dimension of Asanas

Beyond their physical benefits, asanas hold profound spiritual significance. Each posture is a sacred form that channels divine energy, aligns the chakras, and prepares the body for deeper states of meditation and spiritual awareness.

Enhance your asana practice by integrating Pranayama techniques. Use Ujjayi breath during your yoga practice to maintain focus and deepen your connection to each movement. Coordinate your breath with your asanas, inhaling during upward movements and exhaling during downward movements.

Imagine flowing through a series of yoga poses in a serene studio, the sound of your Ujjayi breath creating a rhythmic symphony that guides your movements. Each inhale lifts you into a new posture, while each exhale grounds you deeper into the present moment. This harmonious dance of breath and movement becomes a moving meditation, connecting you to the divine energy within.

In essence, physical asanas and mindful movement are powerful tools for harmonizing body, mind, and spirit. By incorporating these practices into your daily routine, you can create moments of calm, clarity, and spiritual connection amidst the busyness of life. As you embrace the teachings of asanas and movement, may you be inspired to explore the depths of your inner world, awaken to your true nature, and experience the boundless beauty of spiritual awakening. In the sacred space of movement, may you find the peace, clarity, and divine connection that you seek, awakening to the boundless potential that resides within you.

In the embrace of early morning light, the world awakens in a symphony of stillness and potential. The air is crisp, and a sense of sacredness pervades the atmosphere, inviting you to embark on a journey of self-discovery and inner harmony through the practice of yoga and mindful movement. This chapter provides a detailed, mystical experience of integrating yoga and physical movement into your daily life, inspiring you to connect with your body and spirit on a deeper level.

As the first rays of the sun pierce the horizon, you find yourself standing on your mat, ready to greet the day with open arms and an open heart. The world is quiet, and the only sound is the gentle rustle of leaves in the breeze. This is your sacred time, a moment to center yourself and set the tone for the day ahead.

You stand tall with your feet together, grounding evenly through all four corners of your feet. Your spine lengthens, and your shoulders relax away from your ears. As you inhale deeply, you feel the life force of the universe filling your lungs, and as you exhale, you release any residual tension from your body. This simple yet powerful pose roots you to the earth, providing a stable foundation for your practice.

With your breath as your guide, you begin a series of Sun Salutations (Surya Namaskar), each movement a graceful dance of body and spirit. As you reach up towards the sky, you feel a sense of expansion and openness. Folding forward, you surrender to the earth, letting go of any worries or stress. The rhythm of your breath synchronizes with your movements, creating a meditative flow that carries you through each pose.

Example Sequence:

1. **Tadasana (Mountain Pose):** Begin with feet together, grounding yourself.
2. **Urdhva Hastasana (Upward Salute):** Inhale, sweep arms overhead, and look up.
3. **Uttanasana (Forward Fold):** Exhale, hinge at hips, fold forward, and release.

4. **Ardha Uttanasana (Halfway Lift)**: Inhale, lift halfway, extending the spine.
5. **Plank Pose:** Exhale, step back into Plank, engage your core.
6. **Chaturanga Dandasana (Four-Limbed Staff Pose)**: Lower down with control.
7. **Urdhva Mukha Svanasana (Upward-Facing Dog)**: Inhale, lift chest, open heart.
8. **Adho Mukha Svanasana (Downward-Facing Dog)**: Exhale, lift hips up and back.
9. **Step Forward and Repeat**: Step forward to the top of the mat, repeat on the other side.

With each cycle of Sun Salutations, you feel your body awakening, your muscles warming, and your mind becoming more centered. The practice is a moving meditation, grounding you in the present moment and filling you with a sense of vitality and peace.

Transitioning from the dynamic flow of Sun Salutations, you move into a series of heart-opening asanas, designed to expand your chest and stimulate the Anahata chakra, the heart center. These poses invite you to embrace vulnerability and compassion, opening yourself to the flow of divine love.

Kneeling on your mat, you place your hands on your lower back for support. Inhaling deeply, you lift your chest and gently arch your back, reaching your hands back to grasp your heels. Your heart opens to the sky, and your throat extends as you drop your head back. Each breath deepens the stretch, allowing you to release any emotional blockages and embrace a sense of openness and love.

As you hold the pose, you feel a warm, glowing energy radiating from your heart, filling your entire being with compassion and light. The boundaries between your physical body and the surrounding space begin to blur, and you experience a profound sense of unity with the universe.

Returning to a grounded state, you flow into a series of standing asanas that cultivate strength, stability, and focus. These poses connect you to the earth, empowering you to face life's challenges with resilience and grace.

From Tadasana, you step your feet wide apart and turn your right foot out 90 degrees, aligning your heels. Bending your right knee, you extend your arms parallel to the ground, gazing over your right hand. Inhaling deeply, you feel the strength in your legs and the power in your core. Each breath grounds you deeper into the pose, fostering a sense of courage and determination.

As you hold Warrior II, you imagine yourself standing on a mountaintop, the vast landscape stretching out before you. The energy of the earth rises up through your feet, filling you with unwavering strength and stability. This pose empowers you to face any challenges that come your way with confidence and grace.

After exploring the dynamic and grounding aspects of your practice, you come to rest in Savasana, the final relaxation pose. Lying on your back with your arms and legs extended, you allow your body to fully relax and surrender to the earth.

Imagine lying in Savasana, the warmth of the sun gently enveloping you. As you close your eyes and focus on your breath, you feel a deep sense of peace and stillness. Your body melts into the mat, and your mind becomes quiet and serene. In this state of complete relaxation, you experience a profound connection to the divine essence within you.

The practice of yoga and physical movement is a journey of self-discovery and spiritual awakening. By integrating these practices into your daily routine, you can create moments of calm, clarity, and connection amidst the busyness of life. Each asana becomes a sacred form, each movement a prayer, and each breath a bridge to the divine.

As you embrace the teachings of yoga and mindful movement, may you be inspired to explore the depths of your inner world, awaken to your true nature, and experience the boundless beauty of spiritual awakening. In the sacred space of movement, may you find the peace, clarity, and divine connection that you seek, awakening to the boundless potential that resides within you.

In the sacred tradition of Kundalini yoga, physical asanas serve as powerful tools for awakening the dormant spiritual energy coiled at the base of the spine. Known as Kundalini, this energy, when activated, ascends through the chakras, bringing about profound transformation and spiritual enlightenment. The practice of specific Kundalini yoga poses, combined with breathwork and meditation, facilitates the awakening and movement of this energy, harmonizing the body, mind, and spirit. This chapter delves into the mystical role of physical asanas in awakening Kundalini, providing detailed descriptions and examples to inspire and guide your practice.

Kundalini yoga integrates physical postures, dynamic breathing techniques, and meditative focus to stimulate and awaken the Kundalini energy. Each asana is designed to open and balance the chakras, clear energetic blockages, and prepare the body for the powerful surge of Kundalini energy. These practices create a harmonious flow of prana (life force), facilitating the ascent of Kundalini through the central energy channel, or Sushumna Nadi.

Bhujangasana (Cobra Pose)

Bhujangasana, or Cobra Pose, is a heart-opening posture that stimulates the spinal energy and opens the heart chakra, or Anahata. This pose is particularly effective in awakening the dormant Kundalini energy.

Step-by-Step Guide:

1. Preparation:
- Lie face down on your mat with your legs extended and the tops of your feet pressing into the mat. Place your hands under your shoulders, elbows close to your body.

2. Lift and Open:
Inhale deeply and lift your chest off the ground, using the strength of your back muscles rather than pushing with your hands. Keep your elbows

slightly bent and your shoulders away from your ears.

3. Expand and Breathe:
- Open your heart and gaze slightly upward, breathing deeply and feeling the expansion in your chest. Hold the pose for several breaths, focusing on the upward flow of energy along your spine.

Imagine practicing Cobra Pose in a serene garden, the fragrance of blooming flowers filling the air. As you lift into the pose, your heart opens to the sky, and you feel a wave of energy rising from the base of your spine. Each breath deepens this connection, allowing the Kundalini energy to awaken and ascend, filling you with a sense of divine love and compassion.

Ustrasana (Camel Pose)

Ustrasana, or Camel Pose, is a deep backbend that stimulates the heart and throat chakras, enhancing the flow of energy through the central channel and aiding in the awakening of Kundalini.

Step-by-Step Guide:

1. Kneel on Your Mat:
- Begin by kneeling on your mat with your knees hip-width apart. Place your hands on your lower back for support.

2. Lift and Open:
- Inhale and lift your chest, gently arching your back. Reach your hands back to grasp your heels, pressing your hips forward.

3. Deepen the Stretch:
- Allow your head to drop back gently, opening your throat and heart.

Breathe deeply, feeling the expansion and upward flow of energy.

4. Release Gently:

- After a few breaths, release your hands from your heels and slowly return to a kneeling position. Rest in Child's Pose for a few moments to integrate the experience.

Imagine practicing Camel Pose in a quiet forest clearing, the dappled sunlight filtering through the trees. As you open your heart in the pose, you feel a surge of energy rising through your body, stimulating your heart and throat chakras. The Kundalini energy flows upward, creating a sense of openness, clarity, and divine connection.

Example Asana: Sat Kriya

Sat Kriya is a powerful Kundalini yoga practice that combines physical movement, breathwork, and mantra to awaken and channel the Kundalini energy.

Step-by-Step Guide:

1. Preparation:

- Sit on your heels in Rock Pose (Vajrasana). Interlace your fingers with the index fingers pointing straight up. Extend your arms overhead, keeping your elbows straight.

2. Engage and Chant:

- Begin chanting "Sat Naam" rhythmically. On "Sat," pull your navel point inward and upward, and on "Naam," release it. Focus on the movement of energy up and down your spine with each chant.

3. Continue the Practice:

- Continue this practice for 3-11 minutes, maintaining a steady rhythm and focusing on the upward flow of energy.

4. Completion:

- Inhale deeply, hold the breath, squeeze the energy up your spine, and then exhale slowly. Sit quietly for a few moments to integrate the experience.

Example Experience:

Imagine practicing Sat Kriya at sunrise, the first light of dawn illuminating your space. As you chant "Sat Naam" and engage your navel, you feel the Kundalini energy awakening and rising through your spine. The rhythmic movement and mantra create a powerful flow of energy, connecting you to the divine essence within.

Example Asana: Spinal Flex (Sufi Grind)

Spinal Flex, also known as Sufi Grind, is a dynamic movement that stimulates the lower chakras and enhances the flow of Kundalini energy through the spine.

Step-by-Step Guide:

1. Preparation:

- Sit cross-legged on your mat with your hands resting on your knees. Close your eyes and take a few deep breaths to center yourself.

2. Circular Movement:

- Begin making large, slow circles with your torso, moving from the base of your spine. Inhale as you move forward and exhale as you move back.

Focus on the movement of energy along your spine.

3. Switch Directions:

- After a few minutes, reverse the direction of your circles, continuing to breathe deeply and rhythmically.

4. Completion:

- Finish by sitting still with your spine straight, taking a few moments to feel the effects of the movement.

Example Experience:

Imagine practicing Spinal Flex on a quiet beach, the sound of the waves accompanying your breath. As you move your torso in slow circles, you feel a warm, tingling sensation rising from the base of your spine. The movement awakens and energizes your lower chakras, creating a dynamic flow of Kundalini energy.

Physical asanas play a crucial role in preparing the body for the powerful awakening of Kundalini energy. By opening and balancing the chakras, clearing energetic blockages, and enhancing the flow of prana, these poses create a harmonious environment for Kundalini to rise. The combination of physical postures, breathwork, and meditative focus ensures that the energy moves smoothly and safely through the central channel, facilitating profound spiritual transformation.

As you embrace the teachings of Kundalini yoga and physical asanas, may you be inspired to explore the depths of your inner world, awaken to your true nature, and experience the boundless beauty of spiritual awakening. In the sacred space of movement, may you find the peace, clarity, and divine connection that you seek, awakening to the boundless potential that resides within you.

In the sacred tradition of Kundalini yoga, physical asanas serve as powerful tools for awakening the dormant spiritual energy coiled at the base of the spine. Known as Kundalini, this energy, when activated, ascends through the chakras, bringing about profound transformation and spiritual enlightenment. The practice of specific Kundalini yoga poses, combined with breathwork and meditation, facilitates the awakening and movement of this energy, harmonizing the body, mind, and spirit. This chapter delves into the mystical role of physical asanas in awakening Kundalini, providing detailed descriptions and examples to inspire and guide your practice.

Kundalini yoga integrates physical postures, dynamic breathing techniques, and meditative focus to stimulate and awaken the Kundalini energy. Each asana is designed to open and balance the chakras, clear energetic blockages, and prepare the body for the powerful surge of Kundalini energy. These practices create a harmonious flow of prana (life force), facilitating the ascent of Kundalini through the central energy channel, or Sushumna Nadi.

Bhujangasana (Cobra Pose)

Bhujangasana, or Cobra Pose, is a heart-opening posture that stimulates the spinal energy and opens the heart chakra, or Anahata. This pose is particularly effective in awakening the dormant Kundalini energy.

Step-by-Step Guide:

1. Preparation:
   - Lie face down on your mat with your legs extended and the tops of your feet pressing into the mat. Place your hands under your shoulders, elbows close to your body.

2. Lift and Open:
   - Inhale deeply and lift your chest off the ground, using the strength of your back muscles rather than pushing with your hands. Keep your elbows slightly bent and your shoulders away from your ears.

3. Expand and Breathe:

 - Open your heart and gaze slightly upward, breathing deeply and feeling the expansion in your chest. Hold the pose for several breaths, focusing on the upward flow of energy along your spine.

Example Experience:

Imagine practicing Cobra Pose in a serene garden, the fragrance of blooming flowers filling the air. As you lift into the pose, your heart opens to the sky, and you feel a wave of energy rising from the base of your spine. Each breath deepens this connection, allowing the Kundalini energy to awaken and ascend, filling you with a sense of divine love and compassion.

Ustrasana (Camel Pose)

Ustrasana, or Camel Pose, is a deep backbend that stimulates the heart and throat chakras, enhancing the flow of energy through the central channel and aiding in the awakening of Kundalini.

Step-by-Step Guide:

1. Kneel on Your Mat:

 - Begin by kneeling on your mat with your knees hip-width apart. Place your hands on your lower back for support.

2. Lift and Open:

 - Inhale and lift your chest, gently arching your back. Reach your hands back to grasp your heels, pressing your hips forward.

3. Deepen the Stretch:

 - Allow your head to drop back gently, opening your throat and heart.

Breathe deeply, feeling the expansion and upward flow of energy.

4. Release Gently:

- After a few breaths, release your hands from your heels and slowly return to a kneeling position. Rest in Child's Pose for a few moments to integrate the experience.

Imagine practicing Camel Pose in a quiet forest clearing, the dappled sunlight filtering through the trees. As you open your heart in the pose, you feel a surge of energy rising through your body, stimulating your heart and throat chakras. The Kundalini energy flows upward, creating a sense of openness, clarity, and divine connection.

Sat Kriya

Sat Kriya is a powerful Kundalini yoga practice that combines physical movement, breathwork, and mantra to awaken and channel the Kundalini energy.

Step-by-Step Guide:

1. Preparation:

- Sit on your heels in Rock Pose (Vajrasana). Interlace your fingers with the index fingers pointing straight up. Extend your arms overhead, keeping your elbows straight.

2. Engage and Chant:

- Begin chanting "Sat Naam" rhythmically. On "Sat," pull your navel point inward and upward, and on "Naam," release it. Focus on the movement of energy up and down your spine with each chant.

3. Continue the Practice:
   - Continue this practice for 3-11 minutes, maintaining a steady rhythm and focusing on the upward flow of energy.

4. Completion:
   - Inhale deeply, hold the breath, squeeze the energy up your spine, and then exhale slowly. Sit quietly for a few moments to integrate the experience.

Example Experience:
   Imagine practicing Sat Kriya at sunrise, the first light of dawn illuminating your space. As you chant "Sat Naam" and engage your navel, you feel the Kundalini energy awakening and rising through your spine. The rhythmic movement and mantra create a powerful flow of energy, connecting you to the divine essence within.

Spinal Flex (Sufi Grind)

Spinal Flex, also known as Sufi Grind, is a dynamic movement that stimulates the lower chakras and enhances the flow of Kundalini energy through the spine.

Step-by-Step Guide:

1. Preparation:
   - Sit cross-legged on your mat with your hands resting on your knees. Close your eyes and take a few deep breaths to center yourself.

2. Circular Movement:
   - Begin making large, slow circles with your torso, moving from the base

of your spine. Inhale as you move forward and exhale as you move back. Focus on the movement of energy along your spine.

3. Switch Directions:

- After a few minutes, reverse the direction of your circles, continuing to breathe deeply and rhythmically.

4. Completion:

- Finish by sitting still with your spine straight, taking a few moments to feel the effects of the movement.

Imagine practicing Spinal Flex on a quiet beach, the sound of the waves accompanying your breath. As you move your torso in slow circles, you feel a warm, tingling sensation rising from the base of your spine. The movement awakens and energizes your lower chakras, creating a dynamic flow of Kundalini energy.

Physical asanas play a crucial role in preparing the body for the powerful awakening of Kundalini energy. By opening and balancing the chakras, clearing energetic blockages, and enhancing the flow of prana, these poses create a harmonious environment for Kundalini to rise. The combination of physical postures, breathwork, and meditative focus ensures that the energy moves smoothly and safely through the central channel, facilitating profound spiritual transformation.

As you embrace the teachings of Kundalini yoga and physical asanas, may you be inspired to explore the depths of your inner world, awaken to your true nature, and experience the boundless beauty of spiritual awakening. In the sacred space of movement, may you find the peace, clarity, and divine connection that you seek, awakening to the boundless potential that resides within you.

Pillar Four

Introduction to Diet and Nutrition

In the vast tapestry of our existence, diet and nutrition hold a sacred place, weaving the threads of physical health, mental clarity, and spiritual vitality. Just as a well-tuned instrument creates harmonious music, a balanced diet nurtures the body and soul, fostering a deep connection with the universe and the divine essence within. This chapter delves into the mystical role of diet and nutrition in our lives, inspiring you to embrace mindful eating and holistic nourishment as vital components of your spiritual journey.

Food is more than mere sustenance; it is a divine gift, a manifestation of the Earth's bounty and the universe's abundant energy. In many ancient traditions, the act of eating is considered a sacred ritual, a moment to honor the interconnectedness of all life. The choices we make about what to consume are not just decisions about fuel for our bodies but also about aligning ourselves with the rhythms of nature and the cosmos. Imagine sitting down to a meal, the vibrant colors and fresh aromas of the food before you, each bite an offering to the temple of your body. This mindful approach to eating transforms the mundane act of consumption into a spiritual practice, infusing each meal with gratitude and reverence.

In the mystical traditions of Ayurveda and Traditional Chinese Medicine, food is seen as a carrier of prana or qi, the vital life force that animates all living beings. Different foods possess distinct energetic qualities that can either harmonize or disrupt the balance within our bodies. For example, fresh fruits and vegetables are imbued with vibrant, life-giving energy, while processed and refined foods may lack this vital essence. By choosing foods that resonate with high vibrational energy, we can enhance our physical health and spiritual well-being.

Consider the simple act of picking a ripe apple from a tree, feeling its firm skin and vibrant color. As you bite into the crisp, juicy flesh, you are not only consuming its physical nutrients but also absorbing the life force it contains. This awareness transforms eating into a sacred communion with nature, an act that nourishes both body and spirit.

Mindful eating is the practice of bringing full awareness to the experience of eating, savoring each bite, and being present in the moment. This practice not only enhances our enjoyment of food but also fosters a deeper connection to our bodies and the wisdom they hold. By slowing down and paying attention to the tastes, textures, and aromas of our meals, we cultivate a sense of gratitude and presence that extends beyond the dining table.

Imagine sitting down for a meal, free from distractions, and taking a moment to appreciate the food before you. As you eat, you focus on each bite, noticing the flavors and textures, chewing slowly, and savoring the experience. This mindful approach to eating can transform your relationship with food, helping you to listen to your body's signals of hunger and fullness, and fostering a greater sense of balance and well-being.

Balanced nutrition involves a harmonious blend of macronutrients (proteins, fats, and carbohydrates) and micronutrients (vitamins and minerals) that support the body's functions and promote overall health. However, beyond the physical components, there is an alchemical aspect to nutrition that considers the energetic properties of food. For instance, grounding foods like root vegetables can help stabilize and center your energy, while leafy greens and fruits can uplift and cleanse your system.

Imagine crafting a meal that balances these elements: a nourishing soup made with root vegetables like carrots and sweet potatoes, combined with leafy greens and a touch of fresh herbs. This alchemical approach to nutrition creates a meal that not only satisfies your physical hunger but also aligns your energy with the natural rhythms of the Earth, promoting harmony and balance within.

Detoxification and Spiritual Clarity

In many spiritual traditions, detoxification is seen as a way to purify the body and mind, creating a clear channel for spiritual energy to flow. By eliminating toxins and adopting a clean, wholesome diet, we can enhance our mental clarity, emotional stability, and spiritual receptivity. This process often involves incorporating cleansing foods and practices, such as drinking plenty of water, eating fiber-rich vegetables, and avoiding processed foods.

Imagine embarking on a gentle detox, drinking herbal teas, and consuming fresh, organic produce. As you cleanse your body, you feel a sense of lightness and clarity, a renewed connection to your inner self, and a deeper attunement to the divine. This practice of detoxification becomes a sacred ritual, a way to honor and care for the vessel of your body.

The Role of Fasting in Spiritual Growth

Fasting, the voluntary abstention from food, has been practiced for centuries as a means of spiritual purification and enlightenment. By temporarily denying the physical body, fasting allows the spirit to rise and connect more deeply with the divine. This practice can enhance mental clarity, promote introspection, and foster a deeper sense of gratitude and humility.

Imagine undertaking a mindful fast, spending the time you would normally eat in meditation and reflection. As you move through the fast, you become acutely aware of the sensations in your body and the thoughts in your mind. This heightened awareness fosters a deeper connection to your spiritual self, a sense of renewal, and a profound appreciation for the simple gift of nourishment.

A holistic approach to diet and nutrition considers not only what we eat but also how we live. This approach emphasizes the importance of balanced living, incorporating regular physical activity, sufficient rest, and stress management. By aligning our lifestyle with the principles of holistic health, we create a foundation for sustained well-being and spiritual growth.

Imagine crafting a daily routine that includes nourishing meals, regular exercise, and mindful practices such as meditation and yoga. This balanced approach to living fosters a sense of harmony and well-being, creating a fertile ground for spiritual awakening and growth.

In essence, diet and nutrition are integral components of our spiritual journey, providing the foundation for physical health, mental clarity, and spiritual vitality. By embracing mindful eating, balanced nutrition, and holistic living, we can nourish our bodies and souls, fostering a deep connection with the divine essence within and around us. As you embark on this journey of nourishment, may you be inspired to explore the sacred art of eating, to honor the divine gifts of nature, and to awaken to the boundless potential that resides within you. In the alchemy of diet and nutrition, may you find the peace, clarity, and divine connection that you seek, awakening to the boundless potential that resides within you.

In the mystical journey of Kundalini awakening, the foods we consume play an essential role in supporting the body's ability to activate and sustain this profound spiritual energy. Clean eating and detoxification are foundational practices that prepare the body for the powerful surge of Kundalini energy, ensuring a clear and harmonious flow through the chakras. This chapter delves into the specific foods and dietary practices that support Kundalini activation, offering detailed descriptions and inspiring insights to guide you on your spiritual path.

The Sacred Role of Clean Eating in Kundalini Activation

Clean eating is the practice of consuming whole, unprocessed foods that are rich in nutrients and free from toxins. This approach to nutrition aligns with the principles of purity and balance, essential for the smooth flow of Kundalini energy. By nourishing the body with clean, wholesome foods, we create a stable foundation for the energetic shifts and transformations that accompany Kundalini awakening.

Imagine a vibrant garden filled with an array of fresh, colorful produce. Each fruit, vegetable, and herb is a manifestation of the Earth's vitality, imbued with the life force that sustains us. When we consume these foods with mindfulness and gratitude, we absorb not only their physical nutrients but also their energetic essence, enhancing our vitality and spiritual receptivity.

Detoxification is a process of cleansing the body of accumulated toxins, promoting optimal health and spiritual clarity. This practice is particularly important for those seeking Kundalini activation, as it ensures that the energy channels, or nadis, are clear and unimpeded. Detoxification can be achieved through a variety of dietary practices, including fasting, juicing, and consuming detoxifying foods.

Juice fasting is a gentle and effective way to detoxify the body. By consuming fresh, organic juices made from fruits and vegetables, we provide the body with essential nutrients while allowing the digestive system to rest and rejuvenate.

Imagine embarking on a juice fast, starting each day with a vibrant green juice made from kale, spinach, cucumber, and apple. The crisp, refreshing flavors invigorate your senses, and the nutrient-rich liquid floods your body with vitamins and minerals. As you continue the fast, you feel a sense of lightness and clarity, your body and mind becoming more attuned to the subtle energies within.

Key Detoxifying Foods for Kundalini Activation

Certain foods are particularly beneficial for detoxification and supporting Kundalini activation. These foods are rich in nutrients, antioxidants, and natural detoxifiers that cleanse the body and promote the free flow of energy.

1. Leafy Greens:

- Leafy greens such as spinach, kale, and Swiss chard are packed with chlorophyll, vitamins, and minerals. They help to detoxify the liver, alkalize the body, and support overall health. Picture a bowl of fresh, organic salad greens, their vibrant colors a testament to their life-giving energy. Each bite provides a surge of prana, revitalizing your body and preparing it for the flow of Kundalini energy.

2. Cruciferous Vegetables:

- Cruciferous vegetables like broccoli, cauliflower, and Brussels sprouts contain sulfur compounds that enhance the body's detoxification processes. These vegetables support liver function and help to eliminate toxins. Imagine roasting a tray of broccoli and cauliflower, the caramelized edges and rich, earthy flavors nourishing your body and supporting your detoxification efforts.

3. Fresh Fruits:

- Fruits such as berries, apples, and citrus are high in antioxidants and fiber, which aid in detoxification and promote digestive health. Visualize a morning smoothie bowl topped with an array of colorful berries, their sweet-tart flavors and vibrant hues awakening your senses and nourishing your soul.

4. Herbs and Spices:

- Herbs and spices like turmeric, ginger, and cilantro have powerful detoxifying properties. Turmeric and ginger are anti-inflammatory and support liver health, while cilantro helps to remove heavy metals from the body. Imagine a warm cup of turmeric and ginger tea, its golden color and spicy aroma soothing your body and clearing your mind.

5. Hydrating Foods:

- Hydrating foods such as cucumbers, celery, and watermelon help to flush out toxins and keep the body hydrated. These foods support kidney function and promote the elimination of waste. Picture a refreshing cucumber and mint-infused water, each sip hydrating and cleansing your body, preparing it for the influx of Kundalini energy.

The Role of Sattvic Foods in Spiritual Nutrition

In Ayurveda, sattvic foods are considered pure, balanced, and spiritually uplifting. These foods promote clarity, tranquility, and harmony, making them ideal for supporting Kundalini activation. Sattvic foods include fresh fruits and vegetables, whole grains, nuts, seeds, and dairy products such as milk and ghee.

Imagine a meal composed of sattvic ingredients: a nourishing bowl of kichari made with rice, mung beans, and spices; a side of steamed vegetables drizzled with ghee; and a glass of warm almond milk infused with a hint of saffron. This simple yet nourishing meal not only satisfies your hunger but also elevates your spirit, creating a harmonious balance within.

Fasting, the voluntary abstention from food, is a powerful practice for purifying the body and mind, creating a clear channel for spiritual energy to flow. Fasting can take many forms, from intermittent fasting to water or juice fasting, each offering unique benefits for detoxification and spiritual clarity.

Imagine undertaking a mindful fast, dedicating the time usually spent on meals to meditation and reflection. As you move through the fast, you become acutely aware of the sensations in your body and the thoughts in your mind. This heightened awareness fosters a deeper connection to your spiritual self, a sense of renewal, and a profound appreciation for the simple gift of nourishment.

A holistic approach to detoxification and clean eating involves more than just dietary changes; it encompasses lifestyle practices that support overall well-being. Regular physical activity, sufficient rest, stress management, and hydration are essential components of a holistic detoxification routine.

Imagine starting your day with a gentle yoga practice, followed by a nourishing green smoothie. Throughout the day, you take short breaks for mindful breathing and stretching, ensuring that your body remains relaxed and your mind clear. In the evening, you unwind with a detoxifying herbal tea and a gratitude meditation, reflecting on the positive changes you are making in your life.

Spiritual nutrition is not just about what we eat but how we eat. By incorporating mindful eating practices, we can transform our relationship with food and enhance our spiritual well-being. This involves eating slowly, savoring each bite, and expressing gratitude for the nourishment we receive.

Imagine sitting down to a meal, the table set with fresh, wholesome foods. As you take your first bite, you close your eyes and focus on the flavors and textures, chewing slowly and savoring the experience. Each meal becomes a moment of mindfulness, a sacred ritual that nourishes your body and soul.

In essence, the journey of Kundalini activation is deeply intertwined with the foods we consume and the practices we adopt. By embracing detoxification and clean eating, we create a foundation for the free flow of spiritual energy, enhancing our vitality and spiritual receptivity. As you explore the sacred art of spiritual nutrition, may you be inspired to nourish your body and soul with intention and reverence, awakening to the boundless potential that resides within you. In the alchemy of diet and spiritual energy, may you find the peace, clarity, and divine connection that you seek, awakening to the boundless potential that resides within you.

In the vast, intricate dance of existence, our bodies are the vessels through which we experience and interact with the world. They are temples housing the spirit, deserving reverence and care. The practice of detoxifying the body, an ancient and sacred ritual, plays a crucial role in maintaining the sanctity of this temple. Detoxification is more than a physical cleansing; it is a holistic process that rejuvenates the body, clears the mind, and elevates the spirit. This chapter explores the profound importance of detoxifying the body, weaving together detailed descriptions and mystical insights to inspire and guide you on your path to holistic well-being.

Detoxification is the process of removing toxins from the body, purifying it to restore balance and harmony. In our modern world, we are constantly exposed to pollutants, chemicals, and unhealthy foods that can accumulate in our bodies, creating blockages and imbalances. These toxins can disrupt our physical health, cloud our mental clarity, and dampen our spiritual vitality. Imagine your body as a river, the life force flowing freely and vibrantly. When toxins accumulate, they create obstacles and stagnation, obstructing the natural flow. Detoxification acts as a cleansing rain, washing away impurities and restoring the river to its pristine state.

The Physical Benefits of Detoxification

On a physical level, detoxification supports the body's natural processes of elimination and rejuvenation. It enhances the function of the liver, kidneys, and digestive system, which are responsible for filtering and expelling toxins. By incorporating detoxifying foods and practices, we can alleviate the burden on these organs, allowing them to function more efficiently.

Imagine consuming a diet rich in fresh fruits, vegetables, and hydrating fluids, all of which aid in flushing out toxins. Leafy greens like spinach and kale are packed with chlorophyll, which helps to cleanse the blood and support liver function. Citrus fruits like lemons and oranges are rich in antioxidants and vitamin C, boosting the immune system and enhancing detoxification. Herbs like cilantro and parsley act as natural chelators, binding to heavy metals and helping to remove them from the body. These foods work synergistically, purifying the body and restoring its natural vitality.

Detoxification also has profound effects on mental clarity and emotional balance. Toxins can affect brain function, leading to symptoms such as brain fog, anxiety, and depression. By cleansing the body, we create a clearer, more stable foundation for the mind. This clarity allows us to think more clearly, make better decisions, and experience a greater sense of calm and focus.

Consider the practice of a juice cleanse, where you consume nutrient-dense juices made from fresh fruits and vegetables. As your body detoxifies, you may notice a reduction in mental fog and a heightened sense of alertness. Emotional toxins, such as stress and unresolved trauma, may also surface during this process, providing an opportunity for release and healing. This emotional detoxification is essential for achieving a state of inner peace and emotional resilience.

On a spiritual level, detoxification purifies the channels through which spiritual energy flows, enhancing our connection to the divine. In many spiritual traditions, detoxification is seen as a way to prepare the body for deeper states of meditation and spiritual practice. By removing physical and energetic blockages, we allow the life force, or prana, to flow freely through the chakras, promoting spiritual awakening and transformation.

Imagine engaging in a detoxification ritual that includes fasting, herbal teas, and meditation. As you cleanse your body, you feel a renewed sense of energy and vitality. The prana flows more freely, heightening your spiritual awareness and deepening your meditation practice. This process not only enhances your physical and mental well-being but also elevates your spiritual consciousness, allowing you to experience a deeper connection to your true self and the universe.

Detoxification is not a one-time event but a holistic approach to living that involves regular practices and lifestyle choices. It includes adopting a clean, wholesome diet, staying hydrated, engaging in regular physical activity, and incorporating relaxation techniques such as yoga and meditation. These practices work together to support the body's natural detoxification processes and maintain overall well-being.

Imagine creating a daily routine that includes morning yoga, a nutrient-rich smoothie, and time for reflection and meditation. Throughout the day, you stay mindful of your food choices, opting for fresh, organic produce and avoiding processed foods. In the evening, you unwind with a relaxing herbal tea and a gratitude practice. This holistic approach to detoxification creates a harmonious balance in your life, promoting sustained health and spiritual growth.

Detoxification is a sacred journey of self-discovery and renewal. It is an invitation to honor and care for the temple of your body, to cleanse it of impurities, and to restore its natural state of balance and harmony. This process requires dedication, mindfulness, and a willingness to embrace change. Yet, the rewards are profound—a renewed sense of vitality, mental clarity, emotional balance, and spiritual elevation.

As you embark on this journey, may you be inspired to explore the sacred art of detoxification with reverence and intention. May you honor your body as a temple, nurturing it with the pure, life-giving energy of wholesome foods and mindful practices. In the alchemy of detoxification, may you find the peace, clarity, and divine connection that you seek, awakening to the boundless potential that resides within you. In the sacred dance of existence, may your body be a vessel of light and harmony, a reflection of the divine energy that flows through all creation.

Recipes and meal plans for spiritual nourishment.

In the journey of spiritual nourishment, the food we consume plays a pivotal role in harmonizing our body, mind, and spirit. Crafting meals with intention and mindfulness can elevate the act of eating into a sacred ritual, supporting our physical health and spiritual growth. This chapter offers a collection of recipes and meal plans designed to provide spiritual nourishment, using wholesome, natural ingredients to create dishes that are both delicious and energetically uplifting.

Breakfast: Starting the Day with Vitality

Green Goddess Smoothie

A vibrant, nutrient-packed smoothie to kickstart your day with energy and clarity.

Ingredients:
- 1 cup spinach
- 1/2 cup kale
- 1 green apple, chopped
- 1/2 cucumber, chopped
- 1/2 avocado
- 1 tablespoon chia seeds
- 1 cup coconut water
- Juice of 1 lemon
- 1 teaspoon spirulina (optional)

Instructions:

1. Combine all ingredients in a blender.
2. Blend until smooth, adding more coconut water if needed for desired consistency.
3. Pour into a glass and enjoy the vibrant, energizing flavors.

Spiritual Insight:

This smoothie is packed with chlorophyll-rich greens, providing a powerful dose of prana. The addition of spirulina enhances the detoxifying properties, making it a perfect start to your day.

Lunch: Midday Rejuvenation

Quinoa and Vegetable Buddha Bowl

A balanced, colorful bowl filled with wholesome ingredients to sustain your energy through the day.

Ingredients:
- 1 cup cooked quinoa
- 1/2 cup roasted sweet potatoes
- 1/2 cup steamed broccoli
- 1/4 cup shredded carrots
- 1/4 cup sliced cucumber
- 1/4 cup avocado slices
- Handful of mixed greens
- 1 tablespoon pumpkin seeds

Tahini Dressing:
- 2 tablespoons tahini
- 1 tablespoon lemon juice
- 1 tablespoon apple cider vinegar
- 1 teaspoon maple syrup
- Water to thin

Instructions:

1. Arrange the quinoa and vegetables in a bowl, creating a colorful, balanced presentation.
2. Whisk together the dressing ingredients, adding water until the desired consistency is reached.
3. Drizzle the tahini dressing over the bowl and sprinkle with pumpkin seeds.

Spiritual Insight:

The Buddha Bowl is a harmonious blend of flavors and textures, representing balance and nourishment. The variety of vegetables provides a spectrum of nutrients, while the quinoa offers a complete protein source.

Dinner: Evening Calm

Lentil and Vegetable Stew

A hearty, grounding stew that nourishes the body and soul, perfect for winding down after a long day.

Ingredients:
- 1 cup green or brown lentils, rinsed
- 1 onion, chopped
- 2 cloves garlic, minced
- 2 carrots, chopped
- 2 celery stalks, chopped
- 1 sweet potato, diced
- 1 can diced tomatoes
- 4 cups vegetable broth
- 1 teaspoon cumin
- 1 teaspoon turmeric
- 1 teaspoon thyme
- Salt and pepper to taste
- Fresh parsley for garnish

Instructions:

1. In a large pot, sauté the onion and garlic until fragrant.
2. Add the carrots, celery, and sweet potato, and cook for a few minutes.

3. Stir in the lentils, diced tomatoes, and vegetable broth.
4. Add the spices and bring to a boil, then reduce heat and simmer for 30-40 minutes, until lentils and vegetables are tender.
5. Season with salt and pepper to taste.
6. Garnish with fresh parsley before serving.

Spiritual Insight:

This lentil and vegetable stew is grounding and comforting, perfect for nourishing the body and calming the mind. The spices used, such as turmeric and cumin, have anti-inflammatory properties, promoting overall well-being.

Snacks and Beverages

Golden Milk (Turmeric Latte)

A warm, soothing beverage that combines the anti-inflammatory benefits of turmeric with the calming effects of warm milk.

Ingredients:
- 2 cups almond milk (or milk of choice)
- 1 teaspoon turmeric powder
- 1/2 teaspoon cinnamon
- 1/4 teaspoon ginger powder
- Pinch of black pepper
- 1 tablespoon honey or maple syrup (optional)

Instructions:

1. In a small saucepan, heat the almond milk over medium heat.

2. Whisk in the turmeric, cinnamon, ginger, and black pepper until well combined.
3. Bring to a gentle simmer, then reduce heat and let it simmer for 5 minutes.
4. Remove from heat and stir in honey or maple syrup if using.
5. Pour into a mug and enjoy the warm, soothing drink.

Spiritual Insight:

Golden milk is not only delicious but also incredibly beneficial for reducing inflammation and promoting relaxation. The combination of spices and warm milk creates a soothing effect, making it an ideal evening beverage.

Meal Plan for Spiritual Nourishment

Day 1:

- Breakfast: Green Goddess Smoothie
  - Lunch: Quinoa and Vegetable Buddha Bowl
  - Snack: Handful of mixed nuts and a piece of fruit
  - Dinner: Lentil and Vegetable Stew
  - Beverage: Golden Milk before bed

Day 2:

- Breakfast: Overnight oats with chia seeds, almond milk, and fresh berries
  - Lunch: Chickpea and spinach salad with lemon-tahini dressing
  - Snack: Sliced cucumber and hummus
  - Dinner: Stir-fried tofu with mixed vegetables and brown rice
  - Beverage: Herbal tea, such as chamomile or peppermint

Day 3:

- Breakfast: Smoothie bowl with banana, spinach, almond butter, and topped with granola
    - Lunch: Sweet potato and black bean tacos with avocado and salsa
    - Snack: Fresh vegetable sticks (carrot, celery, bell pepper) with guacamole
    - Dinner: Baked salmon (or tofu) with quinoa and steamed asparagus
    - Beverage: Warm lemon water with honey

In essence, the journey of spiritual nourishment through diet is a holistic practice that integrates the physical, mental, and spiritual aspects of our being. By choosing wholesome, natural ingredients and preparing meals with intention and mindfulness, we create a foundation for vibrant health and spiritual growth. As you explore these recipes and meal plans, may you be inspired to honor the sacred act of eating, to nourish your body with the life-giving energy of wholesome foods, and to awaken to the boundless potential that resides within you. In the alchemy of diet and spiritual energy, may you find the peace, clarity, and divine connection that you seek, nourishing your body and soul with every bite.

Pillar Five

Introduction to Sound and Mantras

In the grand symphony of the universe, sound is the invisible thread that connects all creation. It is the primordial vibration that permeates every atom and cell, harmonizing the physical, mental, and spiritual realms. The power of sound lies not only in its ability to communicate and convey emotion but also in its profound impact on our bodies and consciousness. This chapter delves into the vibrational impact of sound on the body, exploring its mystical properties and inspiring you to harness its transformative power for spiritual growth and healing.In the vast symphony of existence, sound is the primordial vibration that weaves together the fabric of reality. It is the unseen force that shapes and sustains the cosmos, resonating through every atom and cell, connecting us to the divine source. Among the myriad forms of sound, mantras hold a special place in the spiritual traditions of the world. These sacred syllables, words, and phrases are more than mere utterances; they are potent vehicles of spiritual energy, capable of transforming consciousness and aligning us with the highest planes of existence. This chapter explores the mystical power of sound and mantras, inviting you to delve into their profound significance and inspiring you to incorporate them into your spiritual practice.

Sound is the essence of creation. According to ancient Vedic texts, the universe began with the primordial sound, AUM (OM), a vibration that set the cosmos into motion. This sacred syllable is considered the sound of the divine, encapsulating the past, present, and future, and transcending time itself. When we chant AUM, we tap into this primordial vibration, aligning ourselves with the source of all existence.

Imagine sitting in a quiet space, the air thick with stillness. You close your eyes and take a deep breath, allowing the sound of AUM to resonate from the depths of your being. As the sound vibrates through your body, you feel a sense of unity with the universe, a profound connection to the divine essence that permeates all things. This simple yet powerful practice can elevate your consciousness, bringing you closer to the ultimate reality.

Modern science has begun to uncover the profound effects of sound and vibration on the human body and mind. Studies have shown that certain frequencies can influence brainwave patterns, promoting relaxation, reducing stress, and enhancing cognitive function. Sound therapy, which utilizes these principles, has been used to treat various physical and mental health conditions, demonstrating the transformative power of sound.

Consider the sound of a Tibetan singing bowl, its rich, resonant tones filling the space around you. As the vibrations wash over you, you feel a deep sense of calm and clarity, your mind quieting and your body relaxing. This is the healing power of sound, a testament to its ability to harmonize and heal at the deepest levels.

Mantras are specific sequences of sounds, words, or phrases that have been used for millennia to invoke divine energies, protect against negative influences, and aid in spiritual growth. Each mantra carries a unique vibrational frequency, resonating with specific aspects of the divine and unlocking different levels of consciousness.

The word "mantra" is derived from the Sanskrit words "manas," meaning mind, and "tra," meaning tool or instrument. Thus, a mantra is an instrument of the mind, a tool for focusing and channeling thought and energy. When chanted with intention and devotion, mantras can transform the mind, purify the heart, and elevate the soul.

One of the most powerful ways to harness the energy of mantras is through the practice of japa, the repetitive chanting of a mantra. This practice can be done silently, aloud, or in a whisper, and is often accompanied by the use of a mala, a string of prayer beads used to count repetitions.

Imagine sitting in a peaceful corner of your home, a mala in your hand, and the mantra "Om Mani Padme Hum" on your lips. With each repetition, you feel the mantra's vibrations resonating through your body, clearing away negativity and filling you with divine light. The rhythmic repetition of the mantra becomes a meditative practice, quieting the mind and opening the heart to the presence of the divine.

In the practice of Kundalini yoga, mantras play a crucial role in awakening and guiding the Kundalini energy. Specific mantras are used to activate and balance the chakras, clear energetic blockages, and facilitate the ascent of Kundalini through the central channel, or Sushumna Nadi.

Consider the mantra "Sat Nam," which means "Truth is my identity." This mantra is often used in Kundalini yoga to awaken the inner truth and align with the higher self. Chanting "Sat Nam" with intention and focus can help activate the higher chakras, facilitating the flow of Kundalini energy and promoting spiritual awakening.

Integrating Sound and Mantras into Daily Practice

Incorporating sound and mantras into your daily practice can be a transformative experience, enhancing your spiritual journey and fostering a deeper connection with the divine. Begin by setting aside a few minutes each day for mantra meditation, allowing the sacred sounds to resonate within you.

Imagine starting your day with the Gayatri Mantra, one of the most revered mantras in the Vedic tradition. As you chant this powerful invocation, you feel the divine light filling your heart and mind, dispelling darkness and ignorance. Throughout the day, you carry this light within you, guiding your thoughts, words, and actions.

To deepen your practice, create a sacred sound space in your home. This can be a quiet corner or a dedicated room where you can meditate, chant mantras, and listen to healing sounds. Fill this space with objects that inspire you, such as a singing bowl, a harmonium, or images of divine beings.

Imagine entering this sacred space, the air filled with the gentle hum of a mantra playing softly in the background. You sit on a comfortable cushion, light a candle, and close your eyes. As you begin to chant, the vibrations of the mantra envelop you, transporting you to a place of inner peace and divine connection.

In essence, sound and mantras are powerful tools for spiritual transformation, capable of harmonizing the body, mind, and spirit. By incorporating these practices into your daily life, you can elevate your consciousness, heal your being, and deepen your connection with the divine. As you explore the sacred power of sound and mantras, may you be inspired to embrace their profound wisdom, to chant with devotion and intention, and to awaken to the boundless potential that resides within you. In the mystical dance of sound, may you find the peace, clarity, and divine connection that you seek, resonating with the sacred vibrations of the universe.

From the dawn of creation, sound has been the fundamental force that shapes and sustains the universe. According to ancient Vedic texts, the universe began with the primordial sound, AUM (OM), a vibration that set the cosmos into motion. This sacred syllable is believed to contain the essence of the universe, embodying the past, present, and future. When we chant AUM, we align ourselves with this primordial vibration, tapping into the source of all existence.

Imagine sitting in a serene, sacred space, the air still and charged with potential. As you close your eyes and intone the sound of AUM, the vibration resonates through your body, from the base of your spine to the crown of your head. This simple act of chanting connects you to the cosmic energy, creating a sense of unity with the universe and awakening your inner divinity.

Modern science has begun to uncover the profound effects of sound and vibration on the human body. Sound waves, traveling through the air, create vibrations that can penetrate and influence our physical and energetic bodies. These vibrations can alter brainwave patterns, promote relaxation, reduce stress, and even accelerate healing processes.

Consider the therapeutic use of Tibetan singing bowls, whose rich, resonant tones are known to induce deep meditative states and facilitate healing. The vibrations from these bowls create a harmonizing effect, aligning the body's energy centers, or chakras, and promoting overall well-being. Imagine lying in a tranquil room, the soothing tones of a singing bowl washing over you, each vibration dissolving tension and stress, leaving you in a state of serene calm.

Chakras and the Vibrational Impact of Sound

The chakras are the body's energy centers, each resonating with specific frequencies that correspond to different aspects of our physical, emotional, and spiritual health. Sound can be used to balance and harmonize these chakras, promoting the free flow of energy and enhancing our well-being.

The root chakra, located at the base of the spine, resonates with low-frequency sounds. Chanting deep, resonant mantras such as "LAM" can help ground and stabilize this chakra, fostering a sense of security and connection to the earth. Moving up the spine, the heart chakra resonates with the sound "YAM," a higher frequency that opens the heart to love and compassion. The crown chakra, at the top of the head, resonates with the highest frequency, "OM," connecting us to the divine and universal consciousness.

Imagine practicing a chakra meditation, chanting the specific mantras for each chakra. As you move through the sounds, you feel the vibrations resonating in their respective areas, clearing blockages and balancing the energy centers. This practice not only enhances your physical and emotional health but also deepens your spiritual connection and awareness.

Mantras are sacred syllables, words, or phrases that carry specific vibrational frequencies. These sounds have been used for millennia in various spiritual traditions to invoke divine energies, protect against negative influences, and aid in spiritual growth. The repetitive chanting of mantras, known as japa, can transform consciousness, purify the mind, and elevate the soul.

Consider the mantra "Om Mani Padme Hum," a revered Tibetan Buddhist chant that invokes the blessings of Avalokiteshvara, the Bodhisattva of Compassion. Each syllable of this mantra has a profound meaning and vibrational effect, helping to purify the mind and heart, and promoting compassion and wisdom. Imagine chanting this mantra with devotion, feeling the vibrations resonating through your being, filling you with a deep sense of peace and compassion.

Sound therapy, also known as vibrational therapy, is a holistic healing practice that uses sound waves to restore balance and harmony in the body. This practice includes various techniques, such as sound baths, tuning fork therapy, and binaural beats, each utilizing different frequencies and methods to promote healing.

In a sound bath, participants lie down while a practitioner plays a variety of instruments, such as gongs, crystal bowls, and chimes, creating a therapeutic soundscape. The vibrations from these instruments penetrate the body, promoting relaxation and healing at a cellular level. Imagine lying in a sound bath, the gentle waves of sound enveloping you, each note resonating with your body's natural frequencies, aligning your energy and promoting deep healing.

The journey of sound is a mystical exploration of the unseen forces that shape our reality. By understanding and harnessing the vibrational impact of sound, we can transform our physical, mental, and spiritual well-being. Sound is not just a tool for healing; it is a gateway to higher consciousness and divine connection.

As you explore the power of sound, may you be inspired to incorporate its transformative energy into your daily practice. Whether through chanting mantras, listening to healing music, or participating in sound therapy, let the vibrations of sound resonate within you, harmonizing your body, mind, and spirit. In the mystical dance of sound, may you find the peace, clarity, and divine connection that you seek, awakening to the boundless potential that resides within you.

In the intricate web of existence, sound emerges as a fundamental force that shapes and influences every aspect of our being. From the earliest moments of creation, sound has played a pivotal role in structuring the universe, resonating through every atom and cell, and connecting us to the divine. The vibrational impact of sound on the body is profound and multifaceted, influencing our physical, emotional, and spiritual health. This chapter delves deeply into the mystical and scientific aspects of sound, exploring how its vibrations affect the body and consciousness, and providing detailed descriptions and examples to inspire and enlighten.

At the heart of many spiritual traditions lies the belief that sound is the origin of all creation. In the Vedic tradition, the universe is said to have begun with the primordial sound, AUM (OM). This sacred syllable is considered the sound of the divine, encompassing the past, present, and future. When chanted, AUM resonates through the entire being, aligning us with the cosmic energy and fostering a sense of unity with the universe.

Imagine yourself in a serene environment, the air filled with a palpable stillness. As you begin to chant AUM, you feel the vibration starting deep within your chest, radiating outwards and enveloping your entire body. This vibration not only calms the mind but also harmonizes the physical and energetic bodies, creating a profound sense of peace and connectedness. The sound of AUM acts as a bridge, linking the finite self with the infinite cosmos, allowing us to experience a moment of divine communion.

Modern science provides fascinating insights into how sound and vibration impact the human body. Sound waves are vibrations that travel through the air and other mediums, creating pressure changes that our ears perceive as sound. These vibrations can penetrate the body, influencing our cells, tissues, and even brainwave patterns. This understanding forms the basis of various sound therapies and healing practices.

One notable example is the use of Tibetan singing bowls. These ancient instruments produce a rich, resonant tone when struck or rubbed, creating vibrations that can be felt throughout the body. Studies have shown that the sound from these bowls can induce a state of deep relaxation, reduce stress, and promote healing. The vibrations from the singing bowls penetrate deeply into the body, aligning the energy centers (chakras) and facilitating the release of physical and emotional blockages.

The chakras are energy centers located along the spine, each associated with specific physical, emotional, and spiritual functions. Sound can be used to balance and harmonize these chakras, promoting the free flow of energy and enhancing overall well-being.

For instance, the root chakra, located at the base of the spine, resonates with the sound "LAM." Chanting this sound creates a low-frequency vibration that grounds and stabilizes the energy, fostering a sense of security and connection to the earth. Moving up the spine, the heart chakra resonates with "YAM," a higher frequency that opens the heart to love and compassion. The crown chakra, at the top of the head, resonates with "OM," the highest frequency that connects us to the divine and universal consciousness.

Imagine engaging in a chakra meditation where you chant the specific mantras for each chakra. As you move through the sounds, you feel the vibrations resonating in their respective areas, clearing blockages and balancing the energy centers. This practice not only enhances your physical and emotional health but also deepens your spiritual connection and awareness.

Mantras: The Sacred Syllables

Mantras are sacred syllables, words, or phrases that carry specific vibrational frequencies. These sounds have been used for millennia in various spiritual traditions to invoke divine energies, protect against negative influences, and aid in spiritual growth. The repetitive chanting of mantras, known as japa, can transform consciousness, purify the mind, and elevate the soul.

Consider the mantra "Om Mani Padme Hum," a revered Tibetan Buddhist chant that invokes the blessings of Avalokiteshvara, the Bodhisattva of Compassion. Each syllable of this mantra has a profound meaning and vibrational effect, helping to purify the mind and heart, and promoting compassion and wisdom. Imagine chanting this mantra with devotion, feeling the vibrations resonating through your being, filling you with a deep sense of peace and compassion.

Sound therapy, also known as vibrational therapy, is a holistic healing practice that uses sound waves to restore balance and harmony in the body. This practice includes various techniques, such as sound baths, tuning fork therapy, and binaural beats, each utilizing different frequencies and methods to promote healing.

In a sound bath, participants lie down while a practitioner plays a variety of instruments, such as gongs, crystal bowls, and chimes, creating a therapeutic soundscape. The vibrations from these instruments penetrate the body, promoting relaxation and healing at a cellular level. Imagine lying in a sound bath, the gentle waves of sound enveloping you, each note resonating with your body's natural frequencies, aligning your energy and promoting deep healing.

The journey of sound is a mystical exploration of the unseen forces that shape our reality. By understanding and harnessing the vibrational impact of sound, we can transform our physical, mental, and spiritual well-being. Sound is not just a tool for healing; it is a gateway to higher consciousness and divine connection.

As you explore the power of sound, may you be inspired to incorporate its transformative energy into your daily practice. Whether through chanting mantras, listening to healing music, or participating in sound therapy, let the vibrations of sound resonate within you, harmonizing your body, mind, and spirit. In the mystical dance of sound, may you find the peace, clarity, and divine connection that you seek, awakening to the boundless potential that resides within you.

The use of mantras in spiritual practices is a profound and ancient tradition that spans various cultures and religions. Mantras, which are sacred sounds, syllables, or phrases, are believed to carry spiritual and vibrational energy that can transform consciousness and connect practitioners to the divine. This chapter explores the historical use of mantras in different spiritual traditions, highlighting their significance and the mystical power they wield.

The Vedic Tradition

The origins of mantras can be traced back to the Vedic tradition in ancient India, where they were first documented in the Rigveda, one of the oldest known spiritual texts, dating back over 3,000 years. In Vedic rituals, mantras were chanted to invoke the gods, seek blessings, and purify the mind and environment. The Gayatri Mantra, a revered hymn from the Rigveda, is one of the most well-known and widely chanted mantras in Hinduism. It is considered a powerful invocation of the sun god, Savitur, and is believed to illuminate the mind and soul of the practitioner.

Imagine a Vedic priest standing by a sacred fire, reciting the Gayatri Mantra with deep reverence. The rhythmic chanting of the mantra, combined with the offering of ghee and other sacred substances into the fire, creates a powerful spiritual atmosphere. The vibrations of the mantra resonate through the environment, invoking the divine presence and blessing the participants with spiritual light and wisdom.

In Buddhism, mantras play a central role in meditation and ritual practices. The repetition of mantras, known as "mantra recitation" or "mantra chanting," is used to focus the mind, cultivate mindfulness, and invoke the blessings of enlightened beings. One of the most famous Buddhist mantras is "Om Mani Padme Hum," associated with Avalokiteshvara, the Bodhisattva of Compassion. This mantra is believed to encapsulate the essence of compassion and wisdom and is chanted by practitioners to develop these qualities within themselves.

Consider a Tibetan monastery, where monks gather in the early morning hours to chant "Om Mani Padme Hum." The deep, resonant voices of the monks fill the temple, creating a harmonious and sacred soundscape. As the mantra is repeated, the vibrations permeate the surroundings, fostering a sense of peace and compassion among the practitioners. This collective chanting creates a powerful spiritual field that benefits not only the monks but also the broader community.

Tantric Practices

In the Tantric traditions of Hinduism and Buddhism, mantras are used as potent tools for spiritual transformation and awakening. Tantric mantras, often referred to as "seed syllables" or "bija mantras," are believed to contain the essence of specific deities or cosmic principles. These mantras are used in combination with visualization, breath control, and physical postures to awaken and direct spiritual energy within the practitioner.

For example, in Kundalini Yoga, the mantra "Sat Nam" is used to awaken the Kundalini energy that lies dormant at the base of the spine. "Sat" means "truth," and "Nam" means "name" or "identity," thus the mantra translates to "Truth is my identity." By chanting this mantra, practitioners seek to align themselves with their highest truth and awaken their spiritual potential.

Imagine a Kundalini Yoga class, where participants sit in a circle, eyes closed, and hands in a mudra (sacred hand gesture). As they chant "Sat Nam," they focus on the sound and vibration of the mantra, feeling it resonate in their bodies and minds. The collective energy of the group amplifies the power of the mantra, creating a profound sense of unity and spiritual awakening.

Sufi Chanting

In the mystical Islamic tradition of Sufism, mantras, known as "dhikr" or "remembrance," are used to remember and connect with God. Sufi practitioners chant the names of God or short phrases, such as "La ilaha illallah" (There is no god but God), in a rhythmic and repetitive manner. This practice is intended to purify the heart, deepen spiritual awareness, and foster a direct connection with the divine.

Visualize a Sufi gathering, where devotees sit in a circle, swaying gently as they chant "La ilaha illallah." The rhythmic repetition of the mantra, accompanied by the beating of drums and the strumming of instruments, creates a powerful spiritual rhythm. The vibrations of the mantra penetrate the hearts of the practitioners, dissolving ego and fostering a profound sense of divine presence and love.

In contemporary spiritual practices, mantras continue to play a significant role in meditation, healing, and personal transformation. In the modern yoga movement, mantras are often integrated into asana (posture) practice, meditation, and sound healing sessions. The popularity of kirtan, a form of call-and-response chanting, has brought the power of mantras to a global audience, allowing people of all backgrounds to experience their transformative effects.

Imagine a modern yoga studio filled with practitioners sitting cross-legged, eyes closed, as a kirtan leader strums a harmonium and leads the group in chanting the mantra "Hare Krishna, Hare Krishna, Krishna Krishna, Hare Hare." The joyful and uplifting vibrations of the mantra fill the room, creating an atmosphere of devotion and unity. Participants feel a deep sense of connection to themselves, each other, and the divine, experiencing the timeless power of mantras in a contemporary setting.

The historical use of mantras in spiritual practices reflects their enduring significance and transformative power. Across various cultures and traditions, mantras have been used to invoke the divine, purify the mind, and facilitate spiritual growth. By understanding and incorporating mantras into our own practices, we can tap into their profound vibrational energy, harmonizing our body, mind, and spirit, and awakening to our highest potential. As you explore the sacred world of mantras, may you be inspired to chant with devotion and intention, experiencing the deep peace, clarity, and divine connection that these ancient sounds bestow.

In the vast and intricate tapestry of spiritual practice, chanting and mantra recitation stand out as powerful tools for transforming consciousness and awakening the dormant spiritual energy known as Kundalini. The specific vibrations of mantras resonate deeply within the body and mind, clearing energetic blockages and facilitating the free flow of divine energy. This chapter delves into the practice of chanting and mantra recitation, focusing on specific mantras for Kundalini awakening, providing detailed descriptions and examples to inspire and guide your spiritual journey.

The Power of Mantra Chanting

Mantra chanting is a time-honored practice that involves the rhythmic repetition of sacred sounds, words, or phrases. Each mantra carries a unique vibrational frequency that can affect the mind, body, and spirit. When chanted with intention and devotion, mantras can purify the mind, harmonize the chakras, and awaken the Kundalini energy that lies coiled at the base of the spine.

Imagine sitting in a quiet, sacred space, the air filled with the subtle fragrance of incense. As you begin to chant a mantra, you feel the vibrations resonating in your body, creating a sense of peace and clarity. The repetitive nature of the chanting helps to quiet the mind, allowing you to enter a meditative state and connect with the divine energy within and around you.

Specific Mantras for Kundalini Awakening

1. Sat Nam
   - Meaning: "Truth is my identity"
   - Description: "Sat Nam" is a foundational mantra in Kundalini Yoga, often used to awaken the Kundalini energy and align with one's true self. "Sat" means "truth," and "Nam" means "name" or "identity." By chanting "Sat Nam," you affirm your connection to the ultimate truth and divine essence within you.
   - Example Practice: Sit in a comfortable meditative posture, close your eyes, and bring your awareness to your breath. Begin to chant "Sat Nam," focusing on the sound and vibration of the mantra. Feel the energy rising from the base of your spine as you chant, creating a sense of alignment and connection with your higher self.

2. Ong Namo Guru Dev Namo
   - Meaning: "I bow to the Creative Wisdom, I bow to the Divine Teacher

within"

- Description: This mantra is traditionally used to open a Kundalini Yoga practice. It connects you to the divine wisdom and guidance within, creating a protective and sacred space for your practice. "Ong" represents the creative energy of the universe, "Namo" means "I bow," "Guru" means "teacher" or "wisdom," and "Dev" means "divine."

- Example Practice: At the beginning of your Kundalini Yoga session, sit in a meditative posture and place your hands in prayer position at your heart. Chant "Ong Namo Guru Dev Namo" three times, feeling the vibration of each syllable resonating through your body. This practice sets the intention for your session and invokes the guidance and protection of the divine teacher within.

3. Har Har Har Har Gobinday

- Meaning: A mantra that invokes the creative and protective aspects of the divine

- Description: This mantra calls upon the divine qualities of creativity, protection, and guidance. It is known for its power to break through obstacles and support the awakening and flow of Kundalini energy. "Har" is a name of God representing the creative aspect, and "Gobinday" invokes the protective and guiding aspects.

- Example Practice: Sit in a comfortable posture and begin chanting "Har Har Har Har Gobinday." Focus on the rhythmic repetition of the mantra and feel the energy it generates. Visualize the divine qualities of creativity and protection surrounding you, breaking through any barriers to your spiritual growth.

4. Wahe Guru

- Meaning: "Ecstasy is the consciousness that brings us from darkness to light"

- Description: "Wahe Guru" is an exclamation of awe and ecstasy, celebrating the divine wisdom that guides us from ignorance to enlightenment. This mantra is often chanted to invoke a state of bliss and heightened awareness, supporting the flow of Kundalini energy.

- Example Practice: Close your eyes and take a few deep breaths. Begin to chant "Wahe Guru," allowing the sound to resonate deeply within you. As you chant, feel a sense of joy and connection to the divine wisdom guiding your path. Allow the mantra to elevate your consciousness and awaken the divine energy within.

The Practice of Japa: Repetition of Mantras

Japa, the repetitive chanting of a mantra, is a powerful practice for deepening your connection to the mantra's vibrational energy. This practice can be done silently, aloud, or in a whisper, often accompanied by the use of a mala, a string of prayer beads used to count repetitions.

Imagine sitting in a peaceful corner of your home, a mala in your hand, and the mantra "Sat Nam" on your lips. With each repetition, you feel the mantra's vibrations resonating through your body, clearing away negativity and filling you with divine light. The rhythmic repetition of the mantra becomes a meditative practice, quieting the mind and opening the heart to the presence of the divine.

To deepen your mantra practice, create a sacred space in your home where you can chant and meditate. This space should be free from distractions and filled with objects that inspire and uplift you, such as candles, incense, crystals, or images of divine beings.

Imagine entering this sacred space, the air filled with the gentle hum of a mantra playing softly in the background. You sit on a comfortable cushion, light a candle, and close your eyes. As you begin to chant, the vibrations of the mantra envelop you, transporting you to a place of inner peace and divine connection. This sacred space becomes a sanctuary for your spiritual practice, a place where you can retreat and rejuvenate.

Integrating Mantras into Daily Life

Incorporating mantras into your daily routine can bring profound benefits, enhancing your spiritual practice and promoting overall well-being. Begin and end your day with a few minutes of mantra chanting, allowing the vibrations to set a positive tone for your day and promote restful sleep.

Imagine starting your morning with the mantra "Ong Namo Guru Dev Namo," setting the intention for a day guided by divine wisdom and creativity. Throughout the day, silently repeat "Sat Nam" to stay connected to your true self and the divine energy within. In the evening, chant "Wahe Guru" to release the stresses of the day and enter a state of blissful relaxation.

The Transformative Power of Mantras

The practice of chanting mantras is a journey of transformation, opening the heart and mind to the divine presence within and around us. As you explore the specific mantras for Kundalini awakening, may you be inspired to chant with devotion and intention, experiencing the deep peace, clarity, and divine connection that these sacred sounds bestow.

In essence, mantras are powerful tools for spiritual awakening and transformation, capable of harmonizing the body, mind, and spirit. By incorporating these practices into your daily life, you can elevate your consciousness, heal your being, and deepen your connection with the divine. As you chant and meditate, may the vibrations of these sacred sounds resonate within you, awakening the boundless potential that resides within. In the mystical dance of sound, may you find the peace, clarity, and divine connection that you seek, resonating with the sacred vibrations of the universe.

Sound healing is a profound and ancient practice that utilizes the vibrational power of sound to harmonize the body, mind, and spirit. Incorporating sound healing into your spiritual practice can create transformative experiences, fostering deep relaxation, emotional release, and spiritual awakening.

This chapter explores various methods and techniques for integrating sound healing into your daily routine, offering detailed descriptions and mystical insights to inspire and guide you on your journey.

The Mystical Power of Sound Healing

Sound has been used for healing and spiritual purposes for millennia, across cultures and traditions. The vibrational energy of sound can penetrate the physical and energetic bodies, dissolving blockages, and restoring balance. When we engage in sound healing practices, we align ourselves with the fundamental vibrations of the universe, creating a harmonious flow of energy that promotes well-being on all levels.

Imagine yourself in a tranquil space, surrounded by the gentle hum of a Tibetan singing bowl. As the bowl is played, its resonant tones wash over you, enveloping you in a cocoon of sound. Each vibration penetrates your body, releasing tension and clearing stagnant energy. This immersive experience transports you to a place of deep peace and connection, where the boundaries between your physical self and the divine essence blur.

To fully benefit from sound healing, it is essential to create a dedicated space where you can engage in these practices without distraction. This space should be serene and filled with objects that inspire and uplift you, such as candles, crystals, and images of divine beings.

Imagine entering your sacred sound healing space, the air filled with the soft glow of candlelight and the gentle scent of incense. You sit comfortably, surrounded by your favorite sound healing instruments—Tibetan singing bowls, crystal bowls, tuning forks, and chimes. This sanctuary becomes a haven for your practice, a place where you can retreat and rejuvenate.

Sound Healing Techniques and Practices

1. Tibetan Singing Bowls

- Description: Tibetan singing bowls produce rich, resonant tones that can induce deep meditative states and facilitate healing. The vibrations from these bowls align the chakras and promote overall well-being.

- Example Practice: Sit in a comfortable position and place a Tibetan singing bowl on your palm or a cushion in front of you. Gently strike the bowl with a mallet to produce a clear, resonant tone. Then, slowly rub the mallet around the rim of the bowl to sustain the sound. Close your eyes and focus on the vibrations, feeling them resonate through your body. Allow the sound to guide you into a state of deep relaxation and inner peace.

2. Crystal Bowls

- Description: Crystal bowls are made from pure quartz crystal and produce a high-frequency sound that can penetrate deeply into the body and energy field, promoting healing and transformation.

- Example Practice: Arrange a set of crystal bowls around you, each one corresponding to a different chakra. Begin by gently striking each bowl, starting from the root chakra and moving up to the crown. As you play each bowl, visualize its corresponding chakra opening and balancing. Feel the high-frequency vibrations cleansing and energizing your entire being.

3. Tuning Fork Therapy

- Description: Tuning forks are precision instruments that produce specific frequencies used to balance the body's energy field and promote healing.

- Example Practice: Hold a tuning fork by the stem and gently strike it on a rubber mallet to activate it. Place the vibrating fork near different areas of your body, focusing on points of tension or discomfort. Allow the sound waves to penetrate deeply, dissolving blockages and restoring harmony. You can also place the fork near your chakras to balance your energy centers.

4. Sound Baths

- Description: A sound bath is a meditative experience where participants are immersed in sound waves produced by various instruments, such as gongs, crystal bowls, and chimes.

- Example Practice: Lie down comfortably in your sacred space and close your eyes. Begin playing your chosen instruments, starting with soft, gentle sounds and gradually building to more resonant tones. Allow the sound waves to wash over you, creating a cocoon of healing vibrations. Focus on your breath and the sensations in your body, letting the sound guide you into a deep meditative state.

5. Chanting and Mantra Recitation

- Description: Chanting mantras involves the repetitive recitation of sacred sounds, words, or phrases, which can elevate consciousness and promote spiritual awakening.

- Example Practice: Choose a mantra that resonates with you, such as "Om Mani Padme Hum" or "Sat Nam." Sit comfortably, close your eyes, and begin chanting the mantra aloud or silently. Focus on the sound and vibration of the mantra, feeling it resonate throughout your body. Allow the chanting to bring you into a state of deep focus and connection with the divine.

Integrating Sound Healing into Your Daily Routine

Incorporating sound healing into your daily routine can bring profound benefits, enhancing your overall well-being and deepening your spiritual practice. Begin and end your day with a few minutes of sound healing, allowing the vibrations to set a positive tone for your day and promote restful sleep.

Imagine starting your morning with a brief sound healing session, using a Tibetan singing bowl to create a peaceful and centered state of mind. Throughout the day, take short breaks to listen to healing music or chant a mantra, maintaining a sense of balance and tranquility. In the evening, conclude your day with a soothing sound bath or a crystal bowl meditation, allowing the healing vibrations to dissolve any accumulated stress and prepare you for a night of restful sleep.

Sound healing is a journey of transformation, opening the heart and mind to the divine presence within and around us. By understanding and incorporating the vibrational impact of sound into your practice, you can harmonize your body, mind, and spirit, fostering deep healing and spiritual growth. As you explore the sacred world of sound healing, may you be inspired to create a practice that resonates with your unique path, experiencing the profound peace, clarity, and divine connection that sound can bestow.

In essence, sound healing is a powerful tool for spiritual awakening and transformation, capable of harmonizing the body, mind, and spirit. By integrating these practices into your daily life, you can elevate your consciousness, heal your being, and deepen your connection with the divine. As you engage with the mystical vibrations of sound, may you find the peace, clarity, and divine connection that you seek, awakening to the boundless potential that resides within you.

Pillar Six

Visualization and Intention Setting

In the mystical journey of spiritual awakening and personal transformation, visualization and intention setting stand as powerful tools that bridge the realms of the seen and unseen. These practices tap into the boundless potential of the mind and spirit, harnessing the creative power of thought and intention to shape our reality. Visualization and intention setting are not merely mental exercises; they are profound spiritual practices that align our inner world with the divine, allowing us to manifest our deepest desires and highest aspirations. This chapter delves into the art of visualization and the power of setting intentions, offering detailed descriptions and inspiring examples to guide you on this transformative path.

The Creative Power of Visualization

Visualization is the practice of creating vivid mental images of desired outcomes, experiences, or states of being. This practice is rooted in the understanding that the mind and the universe are intimately connected, and that thoughts and images held in the mind have the power to influence reality. By engaging in visualization, we activate the creative forces of the universe, aligning our energy with the vibrational frequency of our desires and intentions.

Imagine yourself standing at the edge of a tranquil forest, the air filled with the scent of pine and the gentle rustling of leaves. As you close your eyes and take a deep breath, you begin to visualize a scene of profound peace and serenity. You see yourself walking along a sunlit path, the warm rays of the sun filtering through the trees and casting a golden glow. With each step, you feel a deep sense of connection to the earth and the divine energy that flows through all things. This vivid mental image becomes a powerful tool for grounding and centering your energy, creating a sense of inner harmony and tranquility.

The Science and Spirituality of Visualization

Modern science has begun to uncover the profound effects of visualization on the brain and body. Neuroscientific research shows that the brain cannot distinguish between vividly imagined experiences and actual events, and that visualization can stimulate neural pathways, enhance cognitive function, and promote physical and emotional healing. This scientific understanding aligns with ancient spiritual teachings, which have long recognized the power of visualization as a tool for manifesting desires and achieving spiritual goals.

Consider the practice of athletes who use visualization to enhance their performance. By mentally rehearsing their routines and visualizing success, they create neural pathways that improve muscle memory and increase confidence. Similarly, spiritual practitioners use visualization to align their energy with their highest aspirations, creating a mental blueprint for success and transformation. This practice not only enhances their ability to achieve their goals but also fosters a deep sense of empowerment and connection to the divine.

Intention setting is the practice of consciously directing your thoughts and energy towards specific goals or desires. This practice is based on the understanding that thoughts are powerful forms of energy that can influence reality. By setting clear and focused intentions, we align our energy with the vibrational frequency of our desires, creating a magnetic field that attracts opportunities, resources, and experiences that support our goals.

Imagine sitting in a quiet space, a candle flickering softly before you. As you close your eyes and take a deep breath, you begin to focus on a specific intention—a desire to cultivate greater compassion, for example. You visualize yourself embodying this quality, feeling a deep sense of love and understanding for all beings. As you hold this image in your mind, you repeat a simple affirmation: "I am filled with compassion and understanding." This focused intention becomes a powerful tool for personal transformation, aligning your thoughts and energy with the vibrational frequency of compassion.

To deepen the practice of intention setting, it is helpful to create a ritual that infuses the process with a sense of sacredness and reverence. This ritual can be as simple or elaborate as you wish, incorporating elements that resonate with your personal spiritual practice.

Consider a monthly intention-setting ritual that aligns with the lunar cycle. On the night of the new moon, you create a sacred space in your home, lighting candles and incense, and placing meaningful objects such as crystals, flowers, or spiritual symbols on an altar. You sit quietly, reflecting on your desires and aspirations for the coming month. As you write down your intentions on a piece of paper, you visualize them coming to fruition, feeling the emotions and sensations associated with their manifestation. You may choose to say a prayer or chant a mantra, infusing your intentions with divine energy and support. This ritual not only strengthens your intentions but also creates a powerful energetic imprint that aligns with the natural cycles of the universe.

Incorporating visualization and intention setting into your daily routine can bring profound benefits, enhancing your overall well-being and supporting your spiritual growth. Begin your day with a few minutes of visualization, imagining yourself moving through the day with ease, grace, and purpose.

Throughout the day, take short breaks to reaffirm your intentions, repeating affirmations or visualizing your desired outcomes.

Imagine starting your morning with a brief visualization practice. As you sit quietly, you visualize yourself accomplishing your goals, interacting with others with kindness and compassion, and moving through the day with confidence and clarity. This mental rehearsal sets a positive tone for your day, aligning your energy with your highest aspirations. Throughout the day, you take a few moments to reaffirm your intentions, silently repeating affirmations or visualizing your desired outcomes. This practice keeps you focused and centered, allowing you to navigate challenges with grace and resilience.

The practices of visualization and intention setting are powerful tools for personal and spiritual transformation. By harnessing the creative power of the mind and aligning our thoughts and energy with our deepest desires, we can manifest our dreams and achieve our highest potential. These practices not only enhance our ability to achieve our goals but also foster a deep sense of connection to the divine and the boundless potential within us.

As you explore the art of visualization and the power of setting intentions, may you be inspired to create a practice that resonates with your unique path. May you harness the creative power of your mind to shape your reality and align your energy with your highest aspirations. In the mystical journey of visualization and intention setting, may you find the peace, clarity, and divine connection that you seek, awakening to the boundless potential that resides within you.

Visualization is a powerful spiritual practice that utilizes the mind's eye to create vivid images and experiences, aligning thoughts and energy with desired outcomes. This mystical journey into the art of visualization will explore various techniques that can enhance your spiritual practice, deepen your connection with the divine, and help manifest your highest aspirations. Through detailed descriptions and inspirational guidance, this chapter will illuminate the profound potential of visualization techniques.

Visualization begins with creating a clear and receptive mental space, much like an artist prepares a canvas before painting. To begin, find a quiet and comfortable place where you can sit or lie down without distractions. Close your eyes and take several deep, calming breaths, allowing your mind to settle and your body to relax. As you breathe, imagine a blank canvas or a clear blue sky in your mind's eye, free from any thoughts or images. This mental canvas will serve as the foundation for your visualization practice, providing a neutral and open space for your inner creations to unfold.

Guided visualization involves following a narrative or script that leads you through a series of mental images and experiences. This technique can be particularly powerful for beginners or those seeking to explore specific themes or goals. One of the most popular guided visualizations is the journey to a sacred garden, a personal sanctuary where you can find peace, healing, and spiritual insight.

Imagine yourself standing at the entrance of a lush, vibrant garden. As you step through the gate, you are greeted by the gentle scent of blooming flowers and the soothing sound of a nearby stream. The path before you is lined with colorful blossoms and soft, green grass. As you walk deeper into the garden, you notice a serene pond surrounded by ancient trees, their branches swaying gently in the breeze. You find a comfortable spot by the pond, sit down, and close your eyes. In this sacred space, you feel a profound sense of peace and connection to the divine. You can use this visualization to seek guidance, release stress, or simply bask in the healing energy of your inner sanctuary.

Manifestation visualization focuses on imagining and feeling the experience of achieving a specific goal or desire. This technique harnesses the power of intention and belief, aligning your thoughts and energy with the vibrational frequency of your desired outcome.

Begin by clearly defining your goal or desire. It could be anything from achieving a personal milestone to cultivating a specific quality or state of being. Once you have your goal in mind, close your eyes and visualize it as if it has already been achieved. Imagine every detail vividly—the sights, sounds, smells, and feelings associated with your success. For example, if your goal is to find inner peace, visualize yourself in a serene environment, perhaps sitting by a tranquil lake at sunrise. Feel the warmth of the sun on your skin, hear the gentle lapping of the water, and sense the deep calm within you. The more vividly and emotionally you can imagine your desired outcome, the more powerful the visualization will be.

Healing visualization uses the mind's power to support physical, emotional, and spiritual healing. One effective technique is the Golden Light Visualization, which involves imagining a healing light enveloping and penetrating your body, bringing warmth, comfort, and restoration.

Begin by finding a comfortable position and closing your eyes. Take several deep breaths, allowing your body to relax completely. Visualize a golden light above your head, radiating warmth and divine energy. As you breathe in, imagine this golden light entering your body through the crown of your head, slowly filling every part of your being. See the light moving down through your head, neck, shoulders, and arms, illuminating and healing every cell and tissue. Feel it moving through your chest, abdomen, and back, bringing peace and balance to your organs and systems. Allow the light to flow down your legs and into your feet, grounding you to the earth. As you bask in this golden glow, feel a deep sense of healing and renewal, knowing that the divine energy is restoring you to perfect health and harmony.

Connecting with the divine through visualization can deepen your spiritual practice and foster a profound sense of unity and love. This technique involves visualizing a divine presence, such as a deity, guide, or ascended master, and opening yourself to receive their wisdom and blessings.

Begin by choosing a divine presence that resonates with you, such as a beloved spiritual figure or an abstract representation of divine energy. Close your eyes and take several deep breaths, creating a calm and open mental space. Visualize this divine presence before you, radiating love, light, and wisdom. Imagine a soft, glowing aura surrounding them, and feel their energy extending towards you, enveloping you in a warm, loving embrace. Open your heart and mind to receive their messages, guidance, and blessings. You may ask questions, express gratitude, or simply sit in silent communion with the divine. Allow this sacred encounter to deepen your sense of connection and inspire your spiritual journey.

Incorporating Visualization into Daily Practice

To fully harness the power of visualization, it is beneficial to incorporate these techniques into your daily routine. Begin each day with a brief visualization session, setting a positive and focused intention for the day ahead. Use guided visualizations to explore specific themes or goals, and practice manifestation visualization to align your energy with your deepest desires. Healing visualizations can be used whenever you feel the need for physical or emotional support, and visualizations for spiritual connection can be a regular part of your meditation practice.

Imagine starting your morning with a peaceful visualization, such as the Sacred Garden journey. As you move through your day, take short breaks to reaffirm your intentions and visualize your desired outcomes. In the evening, use healing visualizations to release any accumulated stress and restore your balance. Regular practice will strengthen your visualization skills and enhance your ability to manifest your dreams and connect with the divine.

Visualization is a powerful tool for spiritual growth and personal transformation. By engaging the mind's eye to create vivid and emotionally charged images, we can influence our reality, heal our bodies, and deepen our connection to the divine. As you explore these visualization techniques, may you be inspired to create a practice that resonates with your unique path, experiencing the profound peace, clarity, and divine connection that visualization can bestow. In the mystical journey of visualization, may you find the boundless potential that resides within you, awakening to the divine creativity and power that shapes your existence.

In the realm of spiritual practice, visualization stands as a potent tool that bridges the gap between the physical and the metaphysical, the seen and the unseen. It is a mystical art that harnesses the mind's creative power to shape reality, aligning our inner visions with our external experiences. The role of visualization in manifesting spiritual goals is profound, providing a pathway to bring our deepest desires and highest aspirations into tangible form. This chapter delves into the intricate relationship between visualization and spiritual manifestation, offering detailed descriptions and inspirational insights to illuminate this transformative practice.

The Mystical Power of Thought and Imagination

Visualization is rooted in the understanding that thoughts are powerful forms of energy. What we hold in our minds and hearts can influence and shape our reality. This concept is deeply embedded in ancient spiritual traditions and modern metaphysical teachings alike. By focusing our mental and emotional energy on specific images and outcomes, we activate the creative forces of the universe, setting into motion a process that brings these visions into being.

Imagine standing at the edge of a vast, serene ocean. The water is calm, reflecting the golden hues of the setting sun. As you close your eyes, you visualize your spiritual goals—perhaps a deeper connection with the divine, greater inner peace, or the manifestation of a specific spiritual gift. You see these goals as already achieved, feeling the emotions and sensations associated with their fulfillment. This vivid mental image, coupled with the powerful emotions it evokes, creates a magnetic field that attracts the resources, opportunities, and experiences needed to manifest your desires.

To harness the full potential of visualization, it is beneficial to create a sacred space where you can engage in this practice without distraction. This space should be a sanctuary that reflects your spiritual journey, filled with objects that inspire and uplift you.

Imagine entering a room softly illuminated by candlelight, the air fragrant with the scent of incense. You sit comfortably on a cushion, surrounded by crystals, sacred symbols, and images of spiritual guides. This serene environment enhances your ability to focus and deepen your visualization practice, allowing you to connect more profoundly with your inner visions.

The Process of Visualization

Visualization involves several key steps that help to create a clear and powerful mental image of your desired outcome. Begin by identifying your spiritual goals with clarity and specificity. The more detailed your vision, the more effective the visualization will be.

1. Relaxation and Centering:

- Start by finding a comfortable position and closing your eyes. Take several deep breaths, allowing your body to relax and your mind to settle. As you breathe, imagine a golden light surrounding you, creating a protective and peaceful energy field.

2. Creating the Mental Image:

- Visualize your spiritual goal as if it has already been achieved. Engage all your senses to make the image as vivid and detailed as possible. For example, if your goal is to deepen your meditation practice, see yourself sitting in a serene environment, experiencing a profound state of inner peace and connection with the divine. Feel the calmness in your body, hear the gentle sounds of nature, and sense the warmth of the sun on your skin.

3. Emotional Engagement:

- Emotions play a crucial role in the visualization process. Feel the joy, gratitude, and fulfillment associated with the realization of your goal. These positive emotions amplify the energy of your visualization, making it more potent and effective.

4. Affirmation and Intention:

- Accompany your visualization with affirmations that reinforce your goal. For example, repeat to yourself, "I am deeply connected with the divine," or "I experience profound inner peace in my meditation practice." These affirmations align your thoughts and energy with your desired outcome, strengthening your intention.

Visualization is not a one-time practice but an ongoing process that requires dedication and consistency. Regularly revisit your visualizations, reinforcing the mental images and emotions associated with your spiritual goals. This sustained focus helps to maintain the vibrational alignment necessary for manifestation.

Imagine incorporating visualization into your daily routine, perhaps as part of your morning meditation or evening reflection. Each time you engage in this practice, you strengthen the energetic pathways that connect your inner visions with your external reality, bringing you closer to the manifestation of your spiritual goals.

Examples of Visualization Techniques for Spiritual Goals

1. The Vision Board:
   - Create a vision board that represents your spiritual goals. Collect images, symbols, and words that resonate with your aspirations and arrange them on a board. Place the vision board in a space where you will see it regularly, allowing it to serve as a visual reminder of your intentions and a source of inspiration.

2. Guided Visualization:
   - Use guided visualization recordings that focus on specific spiritual goals. These recordings provide a narrative that leads you through a series of mental images and experiences, helping you to deepen your visualization practice and maintain focus.

3. Group Visualization:
   - Participate in group visualization sessions with like-minded individuals. The collective energy of the group can amplify the power of visualization, creating a stronger vibrational field that supports the manifestation of shared spiritual goals.

Visualization is a transformative practice that bridges the gap between the physical and the metaphysical, allowing us to harness the creative power of our minds to shape our reality. By engaging in this practice with clarity, intention, and emotional engagement, we align our thoughts and energy with our deepest desires and highest aspirations, bringing them into tangible form.

As you explore the role of visualization in manifesting spiritual goals, may you be inspired to create vivid and detailed mental images that resonate with your unique path. May you harness the power of thought and imagination to align your inner visions with the divine energy of the universe, experiencing the profound peace, clarity, and fulfillment that comes from realizing your spiritual aspirations. In the mystical journey of visualization, may you awaken to the boundless potential that resides within you, transforming your dreams into reality and deepening your connection with the divine.

Guided visualization exercises are powerful tools that can enhance your spiritual practice, promote relaxation, and help manifest your goals. These exercises use the power of the mind to create vivid, sensory-rich images and experiences that align your thoughts and energy with your highest aspirations. This chapter offers detailed guided visualization exercises designed to inspire and deepen your connection with your inner self and the divine.

Exercise 1: Journey to the Sacred Garden

Purpose: This visualization exercise is designed to create a personal sanctuary for peace, healing, and spiritual insight.

Instructions:
1. Preparation:
- Find a quiet, comfortable place where you won't be disturbed. Sit or lie down in a relaxed position. Close your eyes and take several deep breaths,

allowing your body to relax and your mind to quiet.

2. Entering the Garden:
   - Imagine yourself standing at the entrance of a beautiful, lush garden. Visualize a wooden gate before you, intricately carved with symbols of nature and spirituality. As you open the gate and step inside, you are greeted by the gentle scent of blooming flowers and the soothing sound of a nearby stream.

3. Exploration:
   - Walk along the path, noticing the vibrant colors of the flowers, the soft green grass under your feet, and the warmth of the sun on your skin. Feel the gentle breeze and listen to the rustling leaves and birdsong. Take your time to explore this sanctuary, knowing it is a place of safety and peace.

4. Finding a Spot:
   - As you explore, you come across a serene pond surrounded by ancient trees. Find a comfortable spot by the pond, sit down, and close your eyes. Feel the tranquility of this place enveloping you.

5. Reflection and Healing:
   - In this sacred space, reflect on any thoughts or feelings that arise. Allow the healing energy of the garden to soothe any tension or stress. You may visualize a gentle, golden light surrounding you, bringing peace and healing to every part of your being.

6. Closing:
   - When you are ready to leave, slowly stand up and walk back to the garden gate. As you step through the gate and close it behind you, know that you can return to this sacred garden anytime you need peace and rejuvenation.

Exercise 2: Manifesting Your Highest Self

Purpose: This exercise aims to align your energy with your highest self, cultivating qualities and experiences that resonate with your true nature.

Instructions:
1. Preparation:
- Sit in a comfortable position with your back straight. Close your eyes and take a few deep breaths, allowing yourself to relax completely.

2. Visualization:
- Imagine a beam of light descending from above, entering your body through the crown of your head. This light represents the divine energy and wisdom of your highest self.

3. Forming the Image:
- Visualize your highest self standing before you. See this version of you radiating with light, embodying all the qualities you aspire to—peace, wisdom, compassion, strength. Notice the details of your highest self's appearance, the way they carry themselves, and the energy they exude.

4. Engagement:
- Engage with your highest self. You may ask questions, seek guidance, or simply sit in their presence. Feel the deep connection and the transmission of wisdom and energy.

5. Integration:
- Imagine your highest self merging with you, their light and energy becoming one with yours. Feel these qualities being integrated into your being, enhancing your connection to your true nature.

6. Affirmation:

\- Repeat affirmations that resonate with your highest self, such as "I am wise and compassionate," "I embody peace and strength," or "I am aligned with my true nature." Feel these affirmations becoming true in every cell of your body.

7. Closing:
- When you feel ready, take a few deep breaths, and slowly open your eyes. Carry the energy and qualities of your highest self with you throughout your day.

Exercise 3: Healing with Golden Light

Purpose: This visualization exercise promotes physical, emotional, and spiritual healing by using the imagery of a golden healing light.

Instructions:
  1. Preparation:
  - Lie down in a comfortable position and close your eyes. Take several deep breaths, allowing your body to relax and your mind to become still.

2. Golden Light Visualization:
  - Imagine a brilliant golden light above your head, radiating warmth and healing energy. Visualize this light slowly descending, entering your body through the crown of your head.

3. Body Scan:
  - As the golden light moves through your body, visualize it illuminating and healing each part. See it moving through your head, neck, and shoulders, releasing any tension or pain. Feel it moving down your arms, chest, and back, bringing warmth and healing to every cell.

4. Deep Healing:

   - Allow the golden light to flow through your abdomen, hips, legs, and feet, grounding you to the earth. Visualize any areas of discomfort or illness being bathed in this golden light, transforming and healing them.

5. Emotional Healing:

   - Let the golden light also touch your heart, releasing any emotional pain or stress. Feel a deep sense of peace and love filling your heart, spreading throughout your entire being.

6. Spiritual Connection:

   - As the golden light continues to flow, imagine it connecting you to the divine source of all healing and wisdom. Feel a profound sense of connection and unity with the divine.

7. Closing:

   - When you feel complete, take a few deep breaths, and slowly open your eyes. Carry the warmth and healing energy of the golden light with you, knowing that you can return to this visualization anytime you need healing and renewal.

Exercise 4: Future Self Visualization

Purpose: This exercise helps you to connect with and embody the qualities and experiences of your desired future self.

Instructions:

   1. Preparation:

   - Sit comfortably with your eyes closed. Take several deep breaths, allowing yourself to relax and center.

2. Creating the Future Image:

- Visualize yourself in the future, having achieved your spiritual goals and living your desired life. See this future version of yourself in vivid detail—how you look, where you are, what you are doing.

3. Engagement:

- Engage with your future self. Ask them how they achieved these goals, what steps they took, and what mindset they cultivated. Listen carefully to the insights and guidance they offer.

4. Embodiment:

- Imagine stepping into the body of your future self, feeling what it's like to have achieved these goals. Experience the emotions, confidence, and peace that come with this state of being.

5. Affirmation:

- Repeat affirmations that resonate with your future self, such as "I am living my highest potential," "I am aligned with my spiritual path," or "I embody my true self." Feel these affirmations becoming true in every aspect of your life.

6. Closing:

- When you feel ready, take a few deep breaths, and slowly open your eyes. Carry the energy and insights of your future self with you, using them to guide your actions and decisions.

Guided visualization exercises are powerful tools that can deepen your spiritual practice, promote healing, and help you manifest your highest aspirations. By engaging in these exercises regularly, you can harness the creative power of your mind to shape your reality, align with your true self, and connect more deeply with the divine. As you explore these guided visualizations, may you be inspired to create a practice that resonates with your unique path, experiencing the profound peace, clarity, and transformation that these mystical journeys can bestow. In the sacred realm of visualization, may you find the boundless potential that resides within you, awakening to the divine creativity and power that shapes your existence.

Setting intentions is a profound spiritual practice that involves directing your thoughts and energy towards specific goals or desires. This practice is rooted in the understanding that our thoughts are powerful forms of energy that can influence and shape our reality. Clear intentions act as a guiding star, aligning our actions and energy with our highest aspirations and spiritual goals. This chapter explores the importance of clear intentions and offers methods for setting and maintaining spiritual goals, providing detailed descriptions and inspirational guidance to help you harness the transformative power of intention setting.

Intentions are the seeds of our thoughts, planted in the fertile soil of the universe, destined to grow and manifest into our reality. Clear intentions are vital because they provide focus and direction, transforming abstract desires into tangible goals. When our intentions are clear and specific, we send a powerful signal to the universe, aligning our energy with the vibrational frequency of our desires. This clarity of purpose not only enhances our ability to manifest our goals but also fosters a deep sense of commitment and determination.

Imagine embarking on a journey without a map or destination in mind. You may wander aimlessly, unsure of where you are headed or how to get there. However, when you have a clear destination and a well-defined path, each step you take brings you closer to your goal. Similarly, clear intentions provide a roadmap for your spiritual journey, guiding your thoughts, actions, and energy towards your desired outcome.

Clear intentions also serve as a powerful tool for self-reflection and inner growth. By taking the time to define and articulate our intentions, we gain deeper insight into our true desires and motivations. This process of introspection helps us to align our intentions with our core values and higher purpose, fostering a sense of authenticity and alignment in our actions and decisions.

Setting and maintaining spiritual goals involves a combination of introspection, intention setting, and ongoing reflection. The following methods offer practical and inspirational guidance to help you create and sustain clear intentions, aligning your thoughts and energy with your highest aspirations.

1. Creating a Sacred Intention-Setting Ritual

Rituals infuse our actions with meaning and reverence, transforming everyday tasks into sacred practices. Creating a dedicated ritual for setting intentions can enhance the power and significance of this practice, fostering a deeper connection with your inner self and the divine.

Example Ritual:
  - Preparation:
  - Choose a quiet, comfortable space where you won't be disturbed. Light candles, burn incense, and arrange meaningful objects such as crystals, flowers, or spiritual symbols around you. These elements create a sacred atmosphere that supports your intention-setting process.

- Centering and Reflection:
  - Sit comfortably and close your eyes. Take several deep breaths, allowing your mind to quiet and your body to relax. Spend a few moments reflecting on your core values, desires, and spiritual aspirations. Consider what you truly wish to achieve and why it is important to you.

- Setting Intentions:
  - Write down your intentions on a piece of paper, articulating them clearly and specifically. For example, instead of writing "I want to be more peaceful," you might write "I intend to cultivate inner peace by practicing daily meditation and mindfulness."

- Affirmation and Visualization:
  - Hold your written intentions in your hands and close your eyes. Visualize each intention as if it has already been achieved, engaging all your senses

to create a vivid mental image. Repeat affirmations that reinforce your intentions, such as "I am peaceful and centered," or "I am aligned with my spiritual path."

- Closing and Commitment:
    - Place your written intentions in a special place, such as an altar or a journal, where you can revisit them regularly. Close your ritual with a moment of gratitude, thanking the universe for supporting your intentions. Commit to taking inspired action towards your goals, trusting in the process of manifestation.

2. Daily Affirmations and Visualizations

Incorporating daily affirmations and visualizations into your routine helps to reinforce your intentions and align your energy with your goals. This practice keeps your intentions at the forefront of your mind, enhancing your focus and commitment.

Example Practice:
    - Morning Affirmations:
    - Begin each day with a few minutes of affirmations, repeating statements that align with your intentions. For example, if your intention is to cultivate compassion, you might repeat, "I am compassionate and kind," or "I radiate love and understanding."

- Visualization:
    - Spend a few moments visualizing your intentions as if they have already been achieved. Engage all your senses to create a vivid mental image, feeling the emotions and sensations associated with your success. This practice aligns your energy with your desired outcome, enhancing your ability to manifest your goals.

3. Journaling and Reflection

Regular journaling and reflection provide a valuable opportunity to track your progress, gain insights, and adjust your intentions as needed. This practice fosters self-awareness and helps you stay aligned with your spiritual goals.

Example Practice:
  - Intention Journal:
  - Keep a dedicated journal for your intentions and reflections. Each day, write down your intentions, any actions you took towards your goals, and any insights or experiences related to your intentions. Reflect on your progress, celebrating your successes and identifying any areas for improvement.

- Monthly Review:
  - At the end of each month, review your journal entries and assess your progress. Reflect on what worked well and what challenges you encountered. Adjust your intentions as needed, refining them to better align with your evolving goals and desires.

4. Accountability and Support

Sharing your intentions with a trusted friend, mentor, or spiritual community can provide valuable support and accountability. This practice helps to reinforce your commitment and provides encouragement and guidance from others who share your journey.

Example Practice:
  - Accountability Partner:
  - Choose a trusted friend or mentor to share your intentions with. Schedule regular check-ins to discuss your progress, celebrate your successes, and seek advice or support for any challenges you encounter. This mutual support helps to maintain your focus and motivation.

- Spiritual Community:

- Join a spiritual group or community where you can share your intentions and receive support from others. Participate in group rituals, meditations, or discussions that align with your goals, fostering a sense of connection and shared purpose.

Setting intentions is a transformative practice that aligns our thoughts, actions, and energy with our highest aspirations and spiritual goals. By creating clear and specific intentions, we send a powerful signal to the universe, inviting the support and resources needed to manifest our desires. Through rituals, affirmations, visualizations, journaling, and community support, we can sustain our intentions and cultivate a deep sense of commitment and alignment with our spiritual path.

As you explore the practice of setting intentions, may you be inspired to create clear, powerful intentions that resonate with your true self and higher purpose. May you harness the creative power of your thoughts and energy to manifest your deepest desires, experiencing the profound peace, clarity, and fulfillment that comes from realizing your spiritual goals. In the sacred journey of intention setting, may you awaken to the boundless potential that resides within you, transforming your dreams into reality and deepening your connection with the divine.

Pillar Seven

Community and Support

In the intricate tapestry of spiritual growth and personal transformation, the role of community and support stands as a cornerstone. This pillar underscores the profound truth that we are not solitary beings on our journey towards enlightenment; rather, we are interconnected threads in the grand weave of existence, each of us playing a vital role in the spiritual evolution of the collective. The power of community and support is both mystical and transformative, providing a sacred space where we can share our experiences, gain insights, and find strength in our common pursuit of higher consciousness. This chapter delves into the essence of community and support, offering detailed descriptions and profound examples to inspire and guide you on your spiritual path.

From the dawn of human history, communities have served as the bedrock of spiritual practice and growth. In ancient civilizations, spiritual gatherings were integral to daily life, fostering a sense of belonging and shared purpose. Temples, monasteries, and sacred circles became havens where individuals could connect with others, share their spiritual experiences, and receive guidance from wise elders. This tradition continues in modern times, where spiritual communities, both physical and virtual, offer a sanctuary for those seeking enlightenment.

Imagine a gathering of individuals under the canopy of an ancient oak tree, the air filled with the soft murmur of shared prayers and the gentle rustling of leaves. The community is gathered in a circle, each person a vital link in the chain of spiritual support. In this sacred space, stories of personal triumphs and challenges are shared, creating a tapestry of collective wisdom and strength. The energy of the group is palpable, a powerful reminder that we are all connected by an invisible thread of divine love and purpose.

Throughout history, various spiritual traditions have emphasized the importance of community in fostering spiritual growth and resilience. In Buddhism, the Sangha, or spiritual community, is considered one of the Three Jewels, alongside the Buddha and the Dharma. The Sangha provides a supportive environment where practitioners can learn from each other, share their insights, and collectively strive towards enlightenment.

Consider the serene setting of a Buddhist monastery, where monks and nuns live in harmony, following the teachings of the Buddha. The daily rituals, communal meals, and meditation sessions create a rhythm of shared practice that strengthens individual resolve and deepens collective wisdom. Each member of the Sangha contributes to the spiritual energy of the community, creating a sanctuary of peace and enlightenment.

Similarly, in the Christian tradition, the concept of fellowship is central to the practice of faith. Early Christian communities gathered in homes and catacombs, supporting each other through prayer, shared meals, and acts of kindness. This sense of fellowship provided strength and solace, especially during times of persecution and hardship.

Imagine a small group of early Christians huddled together in a dimly lit room, the flickering light of candles casting soft shadows on the walls. They share stories of faith and perseverance, their voices mingling in a chorus of hope and devotion. This fellowship creates a spiritual bond that transcends individual struggles, uniting them in their collective journey towards divine grace.

The Mystical Power of Shared Experience

The power of community and support lies in the mystical resonance of shared experience. When we come together in a supportive environment, we amplify each other's strengths, wisdom, and spiritual energy. This collective power can accelerate our personal growth, providing the insights and encouragement needed to overcome challenges and achieve our spiritual goals.

Imagine participating in a spiritual retreat, where individuals from diverse backgrounds gather to explore their inner selves and connect with the divine. The retreat offers a variety of practices, such as meditation, yoga, and group discussions, each designed to foster personal and collective growth. As the days pass, a profound sense of unity and camaraderie emerges, creating an energetic field that supports and enhances each participant's spiritual journey.

In this sacred space, you share your experiences and listen to the stories of others, finding common ground in your struggles and triumphs. The collective wisdom of the group becomes a powerful source of inspiration, guiding you towards deeper self-awareness and spiritual awakening. This shared experience reinforces the truth that we are never alone on our path, but rather, we are part of a vast and interconnected spiritual community.

Creating and sustaining a spiritual community requires intention, dedication, and an open heart. Whether you seek to join an existing community or build one from the ground up, the following principles can help you cultivate a supportive and vibrant spiritual network.

1. Intention and Vision:

- Begin by setting a clear intention for your community. Define its purpose, values, and goals, creating a vision that resonates with your spiritual aspirations. This intention will serve as a guiding light, attracting like-minded individuals who share your passion and commitment.

2. Inclusivity and Compassion:

- Foster an environment of inclusivity and compassion, where all members feel welcome and valued. Encourage open dialogue, active listening, and mutual respect, creating a safe space where individuals can express themselves authentically and vulnerably.

3. Regular Gatherings:
   - Establish regular gatherings that provide opportunities for shared practice, learning, and connection. These gatherings can include meditation sessions, study groups, workshops, and social events, each designed to nurture the spiritual growth and well-being of the community.

4. Leadership and Collaboration:
   - Encourage collaborative leadership, where all members have the opportunity to contribute their unique gifts and insights. Rotate leadership roles, involve members in decision-making, and foster a sense of collective ownership and responsibility.

5. Service and Outreach:
   - Engage in acts of service and outreach, extending the support and wisdom of your community to the broader world. Volunteer, organize charitable events, and participate in social justice initiatives, embodying the principles of compassion and interconnectedness.

The Transformative Power of Community and Support

The journey of spiritual growth is profoundly enriched by the presence of a supportive community. By sharing our experiences, learning from others, and contributing to the collective wisdom, we deepen our connection with the divine and accelerate our personal transformation. Community and support provide the strength, encouragement, and inspiration needed to navigate the challenges and celebrate the triumphs of our spiritual path.

As you explore the role of community and support in your spiritual journey, may you be inspired to seek out and cultivate connections that resonate with your highest aspirations. May you find strength and solace in the shared experiences of others, knowing that you are never alone on your path. In the sacred web of interconnection, may you awaken to the boundless potential that resides within you and the collective, transforming your life and the lives of those around you with the power of love, compassion, and unity.

In the vast expanse of spiritual exploration, finding a community that resonates with your personal beliefs and practices can be both a profoundly enriching and deeply supportive experience. A spiritual community provides a sanctuary where like-minded individuals come together to share their journeys, offer mutual support, and collectively seek higher understanding and enlightenment. This chapter explores various pathways and considerations for finding your spiritual community, offering detailed descriptions and mystical insights to inspire and guide you.

A spiritual community is more than just a gathering of individuals; it is a living, breathing entity that nurtures the soul, fosters growth, and provides a sense of belonging and purpose. Within such a community, you can share your experiences, learn from others, and find comfort in the collective energy and wisdom of the group.

Imagine stepping into a serene space filled with the soft hum of meditative chants, the scent of incense wafting through the air. As you look around, you see faces that reflect the same quest for inner peace and spiritual awakening that you hold within your heart. This environment, charged with a sense of shared purpose and divine connection, becomes a powerful catalyst for your personal and spiritual transformation.

Before seeking out a spiritual community, it's important to reflect on your personal needs and preferences. Consider the following questions to help clarify what you are looking for in a spiritual community:

1. Spiritual Alignment:
   - What are your core beliefs and values? Are there specific spiritual traditions, philosophies, or practices that resonate deeply with you?

2. Community Size:
   - Do you prefer a small, intimate group where you can build close relationships, or a larger community with diverse activities and resources?

3. Activity Types:

   - What types of activities and practices are important to you? Consider meditation, yoga, study groups, service projects, retreats, and social events.

4. Location and Accessibility:

   - Are you looking for a local community where you can attend in-person gatherings, or are you open to online communities that offer virtual connections?

There are many different types of spiritual communities, each offering unique experiences and benefits. Here are some common types of spiritual communities and what they typically offer:

1. Religious Congregations:

   - Traditional religious congregations, such as churches, synagogues, temples, and mosques, provide a structured environment for worship, study, and community service. These communities often have established rituals, teachings, and support systems.

2. Meditation and Yoga Centers:

   - Centers dedicated to meditation and yoga offer a focused environment for spiritual practice. These communities often provide classes, workshops, retreats, and group meditation sessions, fostering a deep sense of inner peace and mindfulness.

3. Spiritual Retreats:

   - Retreat centers offer immersive experiences where individuals can disconnect from the distractions of daily life and focus on spiritual growth. Retreats often include a combination of meditation, workshops, nature walks, and communal living.

4. Online Spiritual Communities:

   - Virtual communities provide a flexible and accessible way to connect with like-minded individuals from around the world. Online forums, social media groups, and virtual meetups offer opportunities for discussion, learning, and support.

5. Holistic Health and Wellness Groups:
   - Communities focused on holistic health and wellness often integrate spiritual practices with physical and mental well-being. These groups may offer activities such as holistic healing, nutrition workshops, and mindfulness practices.

Finding the right spiritual community involves exploration, openness, and a willingness to engage with new experiences. Here are some steps to help you on this journey:

1. Research and Exploration:
   - Begin by researching different types of spiritual communities that align with your interests and values. Attend introductory events, workshops, or services to get a feel for the community's atmosphere and practices.

2. Engage and Participate:
   - Once you find a community that resonates with you, actively participate in its activities and events. Engage with other members, share your experiences, and contribute to the collective energy of the group.

3. Seek Guidance and Support:
   - Reach out to community leaders or experienced members for guidance and support. Ask questions, seek advice, and express your intentions for joining the community.

4. Reflect and Assess:
   - After participating in the community for a while, take time to reflect on your experiences. Assess how the community aligns with your spiritual goals and whether it provides the support and inspiration you seek.

1. Plum Village:

   - Founded by Thich Nhat Hanh, Plum Village in France is a Buddhist mindfulness practice center that offers retreats, teachings, and a supportive community for those seeking peace and spiritual growth. The community emphasizes mindfulness, compassion, and simple living.

2. Findhorn Foundation:

   - Located in Scotland, the Findhorn Foundation is an eco-spiritual community that integrates spirituality, sustainability, and personal growth. The community offers workshops, retreats, and residential programs focused on inner transformation and environmental stewardship.

3. Spirit Rock Meditation Center:

   - Situated in California, Spirit Rock is a meditation center that offers teachings in the Vipassana (Insight) meditation tradition. The center provides retreats, classes, and a supportive community for deepening mindfulness and compassion.

The Transformative Power of Community

The journey to finding your spiritual community is a deeply personal and transformative process. By connecting with like-minded individuals who share your values and aspirations, you can amplify your spiritual growth, find support and inspiration, and contribute to the collective energy of the community.

As you explore different spiritual communities, may you be guided by your inner wisdom and the divine light within you. May you find a sanctuary that resonates with your heart and soul, where you can share your journey, learn from others, and experience the profound power of collective spiritual practice. In the sacred web of interconnection, may you awaken to the boundless potential that resides within you and the community, transforming your life and the lives of those around you with the power of love, compassion, and unity.

In the journey of spiritual growth, community plays an indispensable role, providing support, wisdom, and a sense of belonging that enhances and accelerates individual transformation. Spiritual communities, whether they are based in religious institutions, meditation groups, or informal gatherings, create a nurturing environment where individuals can explore their spirituality, share their experiences, and receive guidance from others. This chapter explores the multifaceted role of community in spiritual growth, highlighting its importance through detailed descriptions and profound examples.

1. Providing Support and Encouragement

One of the primary roles of a spiritual community is to provide emotional and moral support. In times of doubt or difficulty, having a group of like-minded individuals to lean on can be incredibly comforting and empowering. Members of a spiritual community often share similar values and goals, which creates a strong foundation of mutual understanding and compassion.

Imagine a member of a meditation group who is struggling with maintaining a daily practice. The encouragement and shared experiences of the group can provide the motivation needed to persevere. This support can come in the form of verbal encouragement, shared tips and techniques, or simply the presence of others who are committed to the same path.

2. Sharing Wisdom and Knowledge

Communities are rich repositories of collective wisdom and knowledge. Each member brings unique insights and experiences, contributing to a broader understanding of spiritual practices and concepts. This shared wisdom can be particularly valuable for individuals who are new to a spiritual path or those seeking deeper understanding.

Consider a study group focused on ancient spiritual texts. The discussions and interpretations offered by different members can illuminate various aspects of the teachings, providing a richer and more nuanced understanding. This collective exploration fosters intellectual and spiritual growth, as members learn from one another's perspectives and insights.

3. Facilitating Accountability and Discipline

Maintaining spiritual practices can sometimes be challenging due to life's demands and distractions. A community provides a structure of accountability that helps individuals stay committed to their spiritual goals. Regular meetings, group practices, and shared commitments create a sense of responsibility and discipline.

For example, a yoga community that meets weekly for practice not only offers a dedicated time and space for yoga but also creates a sense of accountability. Knowing that others are expecting your participation can motivate you to attend regularly and maintain your practice, fostering consistency and growth.

4. Enhancing the Experience of Rituals and Ceremonies

Rituals and ceremonies are integral parts of many spiritual traditions, and their impact is often amplified when performed in a community setting. The collective energy and shared intention of the group can deepen the spiritual experience, making it more powerful and transformative.

Imagine attending a full moon meditation ceremony at a local spiritual center. The group gathers in a circle, chanting and meditating together under the moonlight. The combined focus and energy of the community create a profound sense of unity and connection, enhancing the individual experience of the ritual.

5. Offering Opportunities for Service and Compassion

Many spiritual communities engage in service activities that benefit the broader community. These acts of compassion and service not only help those in need but also provide members with opportunities to practice selflessness and generosity, key aspects of spiritual growth.

Consider a community that organizes regular volunteer activities, such as serving meals at a homeless shelter or participating in environmental clean-up projects. These activities allow members to put their spiritual principles into action, fostering a sense of purpose and connection to the larger world.

6. Creating a Sense of Belonging and Identity

A spiritual community offers a sense of belonging that is essential for emotional and psychological well-being. Feeling part of a group that shares similar values and goals provides a sense of identity and connection that can be deeply fulfilling.

Think of a long-term member of a religious congregation who has attended services and participated in community activities for many years. This individual likely feels a strong sense of belonging and identity within the community, which supports their overall spiritual and personal growth.

1. The Sangha in Buddhism

In Buddhism, the Sangha, or community of monks, nuns, and lay practitioners, is considered one of the Three Jewels, along with the Buddha and the Dharma. The Sangha provides a supportive environment for practicing the teachings of the Buddha, offering guidance, wisdom, and mutual support. The communal life of the Sangha helps individuals cultivate mindfulness, ethical conduct, and wisdom, fostering spiritual growth and enlightenment.

2. Christian Fellowship

Early Christian communities gathered in homes to share meals, pray, and support each other in their faith. This sense of fellowship provided strength and encouragement, especially during times of persecution. Modern Christian communities continue this tradition through church services, study groups, and community outreach programs, fostering spiritual growth and a sense of belonging.

3. The Ashram Experience

In Hinduism, an ashram is a spiritual hermitage or a monastery where individuals live, work, and study together under the guidance of a spiritual teacher. The ashram community provides a disciplined environment for spiritual practice, combining daily routines, rituals, and communal activities that support individual and collective spiritual growth.

4. Contemporary Spiritual Retreats

Modern spiritual retreats offer immersive experiences where individuals can deepen their spiritual practice in a supportive community. These retreats often include meditation, yoga, workshops, and group discussions, creating a space for personal transformation and community building. Participants leave with renewed inspiration and a stronger sense of connection to their spiritual path and to each other.

The role of community in spiritual growth is multifaceted and profound. Through support, shared wisdom, accountability, enhanced rituals, service opportunities, and a sense of belonging, spiritual communities provide the fertile ground for personal and collective transformation. As you seek to deepen your spiritual journey, may you find a community that resonates with your values and aspirations, offering the support and inspiration needed to grow and thrive. In the sacred web of interconnection, may you discover the boundless potential within yourself and the community, transforming your life and the lives of others with the power of love, compassion, and unity.

Connecting with like-minded individuals is essential for building a supportive and enriching community that can enhance your personal and spiritual growth. Whether you are looking for friends, mentors, or fellow seekers, finding people who share your values and interests can profoundly impact your life. Here are several strategies to help you connect with like-minded individuals, each enriched with detailed descriptions and practical examples.

The first step in connecting with like-minded individuals is to clearly identify your own interests and values. This self-awareness will guide you to the right communities and groups where you are likely to find people who resonate with your perspectives.

Example:

- If you are passionate about meditation and mindfulness, look for groups and communities focused on these practices. Knowing what you are seeking will help you find others who share similar passions.

2. Join Local Groups and Meetups

Local groups and meetups are excellent ways to meet people with similar interests. Websites like Meetup.com and local community centers often host events and gatherings on various topics.

Example:
   - Search for meditation groups, yoga classes, or spiritual book clubs in your area. Attending these events regularly will help you build connections with others who share your interests.

3. Participate in Workshops and Retreats

Workshops and retreats provide immersive experiences where you can connect deeply with others. These events often focus on specific themes or practices, attracting participants who share a common interest.

Example:
   - Attend a weekend meditation retreat or a yoga workshop. The shared experience of learning and practicing together can create strong bonds and lasting friendships.

4. Engage in Online Communities

The internet offers a vast array of online communities where you can connect with like-minded individuals from around the world. Social media platforms, forums, and specialized websites provide opportunities for discussion, support, and collaboration.

Example:

- Join Facebook groups or Reddit communities focused on your interests, such as "Spiritual Seekers" or "Mindfulness Meditation." Participate in discussions, share your experiences, and connect with other members.

5. Volunteer for Causes You Care About

Volunteering for causes that align with your values is a great way to meet people who share your commitment and passion. Working together towards a common goal fosters a sense of community and purpose.

Example:

- Volunteer at a local environmental organization, animal shelter, or community service project. The shared mission and collaborative effort create natural opportunities for connection.

6. Attend Conferences and Expos

Conferences and expos related to your interests provide opportunities to meet industry leaders, enthusiasts, and fellow seekers. These events often include workshops, lectures, and networking sessions.

Example:

- Attend a spiritual or wellness conference, such as a holistic health expo or a mindfulness summit. Engage with other attendees, participate in workshops, and explore the exhibitor booths to meet new people.

7. Take Classes and Courses

Enrolling in classes and courses on topics you are passionate about can introduce you to others with similar interests. Educational settings provide structured environments for learning and connection.

Example:

- Sign up for a course on Eastern philosophy, holistic healing, or creative writing. Engage with your classmates, participate in group projects, and attend class discussions to build relationships.

8. Host Gatherings and Events

Hosting your own gatherings and events can attract like-minded individuals to your space. Creating a welcoming and inclusive environment encourages people to connect and share their experiences.

Example:

- Organize a monthly book club, meditation circle, or potluck dinner focused on a specific theme or interest. Invite friends, neighbors, and community members to join and contribute.

Connecting with like-minded individuals is a journey that requires self-awareness, initiative, and openness. By actively seeking out opportunities to engage with others who share your interests and values, you can build a supportive and enriching community that enhances your personal and spiritual growth. Whether through local meetups, online communities, volunteering, or hosting events, the connections you make will provide mutual support, inspiration, and a sense of belonging on your spiritual path.

In this interconnected web of relationships, may you find the companionship and support that nurtures your growth and enriches your life, creating a network of like-minded individuals who share your journey and celebrate your successes.

Building a robust support system is a cornerstone of personal and spiritual growth. It provides a network of individuals who offer emotional, moral, and sometimes practical support, helping you navigate life's challenges and celebrate its triumphs. Such a system involves intentional actions and strategies to connect with people who can contribute positively to your life. This journey of building and sustaining a supportive network involves understanding its importance, identifying key components, and taking actionable steps to nurture these connections.

A support system is not just a safety net; it is a vibrant network of connections that nurture and uplift you. This system can include family, friends, mentors, spiritual advisors, and community members who provide different types of support, such as emotional encouragement, spiritual guidance, and practical help. The importance of a support system lies in its ability to provide emotional stability, fostering a sense of belonging and understanding during difficult times. Imagine facing a significant life challenge, such as a career transition or a personal loss. Having a support system means having people who listen, empathize, and offer comfort, helping you navigate through these turbulent waters.

Supportive relationships also foster personal growth by encouraging you to pursue your goals and offering motivation and constructive feedback. They help you stay accountable and inspired on your path. For example, if you are working towards a personal milestone, such as writing a book or completing a marathon, having friends and mentors who believe in you and celebrate your progress can make a significant difference. Their encouragement and practical advice can keep you focused and determined, even when you face obstacles.

Moreover, a support system enhances spiritual growth by providing guidance and wisdom. Spiritual advisors and mentors can offer insights and practices that deepen your spiritual journey, helping you connect with your higher self and the divine. Imagine being part of a meditation group led by an experienced teacher who offers personalized guidance and shares profound spiritual teachings. This supportive environment can elevate your practice, making it more profound and transformative.

To build a comprehensive support system, it is essential to recognize and include different types of relationships, each serving a unique role in your life. Family members often provide unconditional love and a sense of deep emotional connection. Friends offer companionship and shared experiences, acting as confidants and cheerleaders. Mentors provide guidance and advice based on their experiences, helping you navigate challenges and make informed decisions. Spiritual advisors offer insights that nurture your spiritual growth. Being part of a community, such as a religious group or social club, provides a sense of belonging and shared purpose.

Building a support system begins with self-reflection and identification. Reflect on your current relationships and identify those who already offer support. Consider areas where you may need additional support and the types of individuals who could fulfill those roles. For instance, you may realize that while you have strong friendships, you lack a spiritual advisor. Identifying this gap helps you focus on finding a mentor who can guide your spiritual journey.

Reaching out and connecting with individuals who can be part of your support system is the next step. This may involve rekindling old relationships, joining new groups, or seeking out mentors. Imagine joining a local meditation group or attending workshops and retreats where you can meet like-minded individuals and potential mentors. Taking the initiative to engage in these activities opens doors to new connections.

Cultivating relationships requires time and effort. Invest in regular communication, mutual support, and shared experiences to strengthen these bonds. Schedule regular meetups with friends, participate actively in community events, and maintain open and honest communication with mentors. Setting boundaries and expectations is crucial for maintaining healthy relationships. Clearly communicate your needs and establish respectful boundaries to ensure that your support system remains nurturing.

Reciprocating support is fundamental to a balanced and nurturing support system. Offer your support to others in your network, creating an environment of mutual respect and reciprocity. Be there for your friends and family when they need you, offer your skills and knowledge to your community, and provide encouragement and guidance to those who seek your help.

Maintaining and strengthening your support system is an ongoing process. Regular check-ins, expressing gratitude, engaging in shared activities, and being open and honest in your communication are key practices. Schedule monthly catch-ups with friends or family members to stay updated on each other's lives and provide mutual support. Show appreciation for the support you receive through thank-you notes, heartfelt compliments, or simple expressions of gratitude. Participate in activities that you enjoy with your support network, such as group hikes, book clubs, or spiritual retreats. This creates lasting bonds and fosters a sense of community.

Finally, as your life and needs evolve, so will your support system. Be open to new connections and willing to adapt your network to meet changing circumstances. For example, if you move to a new city, actively seek out new communities and groups to build a local support system while maintaining connections with your existing network through digital means.

Building a support system is a vital aspect of personal and spiritual growth. It involves intentionally creating and nurturing relationships that provide emotional, moral, and practical support. By reflecting on your needs, reaching out to others, and maintaining strong connections, you can cultivate a network that enriches your life and helps you navigate challenges with resilience and grace. As you build and strengthen your support system, may you find a circle of individuals who uplift and inspire you, providing the encouragement and guidance needed to thrive. In this web of connections, may you discover the boundless potential within yourself and the collective, transforming your life with the power of love, compassion, and unity.

In the mystical journey of life, the role of mentorship and guidance stands as a beacon of light, illuminating the path of spiritual and personal growth. Mentors and guides are the wise elders, the keepers of ancient wisdom, and the nurturers of nascent potential. Their importance cannot be overstated, for they provide the insight, support, and encouragement necessary to navigate the complexities of existence and to awaken the dormant divinity within us.

Imagine embarking on a pilgrimage through an ancient, sacred landscape, filled with the echoes of those who have walked the path before you. A mentor is like the seasoned traveler who knows the terrain, the hidden pitfalls, and the secret oases. With their guidance, your journey becomes not only possible but deeply enriching and transformative. They help you understand the symbols and signs along the way, interpreting the language of the soul that is often obscure and mysterious.

A mentor's presence in one's life is akin to that of a guiding star in the night sky. In moments of doubt and darkness, their light provides direction and hope. They offer a perspective that transcends the immediate challenges, helping you to see the larger picture of your spiritual quest. Through their teachings and example, mentors impart the tools and practices that cultivate resilience, wisdom, and compassion. They are the living embodiments of the virtues they teach, demonstrating through their lives the principles they espouse.

Consider the profound impact of historical figures such as Socrates, whose mentorship of Plato shaped Western philosophy, or the Buddha, whose teachings and personal guidance have illuminated the path for countless seekers over millennia. These mentors did not merely impart knowledge; they inspired transformation. They ignited the spark of inquiry and introspection, urging their disciples to seek deeper truths and to cultivate inner enlightenment.

In the context of personal growth, mentors serve as mirrors, reflecting both the strengths and areas for growth within their mentees. This reflection is done with compassion and a deep understanding of the human condition, encouraging self-awareness and self-improvement. They challenge you to stretch beyond your perceived limitations, to embrace the discomfort of growth, and to trust in the unfolding of your unique journey.

Spiritual mentors, in particular, hold the sacred role of guiding the soul's evolution. They possess the ability to see beyond the mundane and to touch the eternal essence within. Their guidance helps align your earthly existence with your spiritual aspirations, creating harmony and purpose in your life. They offer sacred teachings, practices, and rituals that anchor you in the divine, fostering a deeper connection to the source of all existence.

The importance of mentorship and guidance is also reflected in the communal aspect of spiritual traditions. In many cultures, the transmission of spiritual wisdom is seen as a sacred duty, a lineage of light passed from mentor to mentee. This lineage creates a continuity of knowledge and experience, ensuring that the sacred teachings endure through the ages. Whether it is the guru disciple relationship in Hinduism, the spiritual director in Christianity, or the teacher-student dynamic in Buddhism, the essence remains the same: a profound and transformative relationship rooted in mutual respect, trust, and a shared quest for truth.

In essence, mentors and guides are the harbingers of growth and the custodians of wisdom. Their role is pivotal in the journey towards self-realization and enlightenment. Through their guidance, we learn to navigate the intricate dance of life with grace and insight. They help us to awaken to our true potential, to heal and transform, and to walk our path with confidence and purpose. In the sacred relationship between mentor and mentee, the divine unfolds, revealing the boundless possibilities of the human spirit.

As we arrive at the conclusion of this book, it is essential to reflect on the journey you have embarked upon, or are about to embark upon, in the sacred exploration of spiritual awakening and Kundalini activation. This journey is not just a path you walk but a transformation that unfolds within the deepest chambers of your being. It is a journey of becoming—of shedding the layers of illusion and fear, and emerging into the light of your true self, radiant and boundless.

The process of spiritual awakening is both a profound and challenging endeavor. It requires courage, perseverance, and an unwavering commitment to personal growth and self-discovery. The path is often fraught with obstacles, both internal and external, that test your resolve and push you to confront the shadows that lie within. Yet, it is precisely in these moments of challenge that the seeds of transformation are sown. Like the lotus that blossoms in the murky waters, your soul too must navigate through the darkness to reach the light.

Kundalini activation, in particular, is a journey of immense power and potential. This sacred energy, often depicted as a coiled serpent lying dormant at the base of the spine, represents the untapped spiritual force within each of us. When awakened, Kundalini rises through the chakras, purifying and energizing each one, ultimately leading to a state of heightened consciousness and spiritual enlightenment. This process can be intense and transformative, as it stirs the deep waters of the subconscious, bringing to the surface old patterns, emotions, and beliefs that no longer serve your highest good.

It is important to approach this journey with reverence and mindfulness. The awakening of Kundalini is not to be rushed or forced, but rather nurtured with patience, devotion, and a deep respect for the sacredness of the process. Engage in practices that ground and center you, such as meditation, breathwork, and yoga, and seek guidance from experienced teachers and mentors who can support you on your path. Remember, the journey of Kundalini activation is not just about the end goal of enlightenment, but about the transformation that occurs along the way—the shedding of old identities, the healing of past wounds, and the awakening of the divine potential within you.

As you continue on this journey, it is crucial to cultivate a sense of trust in the unfolding process. Trust that you are being guided by a higher wisdom, that the universe is conspiring to support your growth and evolution. Even in moments of doubt or uncertainty, know that every experience is a stepping stone on your path, leading you closer to the realization of your true nature. Embrace the journey with an open heart and a curious mind, allowing yourself to be led by the inner knowing that resides within you.

Take comfort in the knowledge that you are not alone on this path. Throughout history, countless souls have walked this same journey, each one contributing to the collective awakening of humanity. In this sense, you are part of a greater tapestry of consciousness, woven together by the threads of shared experience and universal truth. Connect with like-minded individuals, build a support system that nurtures your growth, and seek out communities that resonate with your spiritual aspirations. The power of community and shared purpose can amplify your journey, providing the encouragement and inspiration needed to stay the course.

In closing, I encourage you to embark on this journey with courage and commitment. Embrace the unknown, trust in the process, and surrender to the divine flow of life. Remember that the journey of spiritual awakening and Kundalini activation is not a destination but a lifelong adventure—a continuous unfolding of the soul's potential, a dance with the divine. As you walk this path, may you discover the boundless light within you, and may you awaken to the truth of who you are—an infinite being of love, wisdom, and divine power.

May this book serve as a guide and companion on your journey, offering insights, practices, and encouragement as you navigate the sacred terrain of your inner world. May you find the strength to face the challenges, the wisdom to learn from every experience, and the grace to embrace the beauty of your unfolding transformation. As you continue on this path, may you be blessed with peace, clarity, and a deep sense of connection to the divine essence that resides within you. In the sacred dance of life, may you awaken to the infinite possibilities that await you, and may your journey be one of joy, love, and profound spiritual fulfillment.